models. I was in San Francisco and was called back and told by [assistant superintendent Harold] Reasby, "The superintendent says you are to be here for a desegregation briefing."

Moberly called me and Dyksterhuis and Page [James Page, a desegregation planner] in on a Saturday, along with about fifteen other people, all top administrators, and Moberly threw the plan on the table and said, "This is a bunch of trash." He had never read the stuff. He tore into me for fifteen minutes. I got pretty angry and started yelling.[30]

David Moberly and William Maynard did not work well together, and this fact provided some of the dynamics associated with efforts to develop a comprehensive desegregation plan for Seattle.

However, during the fall of 1976, Maynard met twice with the School Board in a retreat setting to develop the criteria that would be used in desegregation planning. It was still assumed by most of the Board members and the superintendent that the plan Maynard was working on would employ only voluntary student transfer strategies.

The Magnet Plan was developed in Seattle during the 1976–77 school year for implementation in the 1977–78 school year. Superintendent Moberly felt that schools could successfully be desegregated with this voluntary approach, and by January the superintendent had told William Maynard that he was to limit his desegregation planning to a voluntary, magnet plan. Moberly had laid down even narrower ground rules than the School Board, and Maynard was ready to quit. Though the School Board's instructions did not permit mandatory strategies, the range of voluntary strategies was further limited by Moberly in his instructions to Maynard.

William Maynard did not resign, but the District-Wide Advisory Committee wanted to find out what was going on. Dan Levant had chaired the District-Wide Advisory Committee on Desegregation (DWAC) since its inception (see Chapter 3). The School Board was invited to an evening meeting with members of DWAC and the Central Area School Council on January 3, 1977, because the committees were convinced that the proposed all-voluntary Magnet Plan would not desegregate the schools, and they wanted to know what the superintendent's limits were, as defined by the School Board. Don Olson recalls the meeting:

On Monday evening, January 3, 1977, a public meeting was held by DWAC, with Dan Levant as presiding president. The School Board and Maynard were invited.

In the course of the January 3rd meeting, Maynard made a statement that he had been directed by Moberly to confine desegregation planning to the magnet school program for the 1977-78 school year. This came as a complete surprise to Board members at the meeting. But the accuracy of that statement was confirmed in a day or two by talks with Moberly.

The understanding between Board members and Moberly had been that desegregation was to occur by voluntary means. However, most, if not all, Board members defined voluntary means to include the redrawing of school boundary lines and the pairing of schools, as well as the establishment of the magnet program. It was a total surprise to learn this was not administration thinking. Also it was quickly apparent that there was insufficient time left to develop additional strategies for the 1977-78 school year.[31]

In January of 1977 the School Board was reluctant to tackle mandatory desegregation; the superintendent was even more reluctant. Desegregation was to continue by voluntary methods only.

The Magnet Plan pointed out the problem that the School Board's goals did not define failure of voluntary efforts. It was possible that every schoolchild in Seattle could transfer to a different school in the district, and there would still be schools which were minority impacted. A goal of recruiting a thousand students each year for three years was set for magnet school recruitment. By May 1977, fifteen hundred students had been recruited to attend magnet schools, but the racial percentages in some of the city's severely segregated schools were not improved much.[32] Where magnet school programs kept students separated from the regular school population, in-building segregation was beginning to be noted.

By May the desegregation office had established a technical planning team, initially to work on a "contingency plan" (possibly mandatory backups) for the voluntary magnet effort. Patte Poc, secretary to DWAC, was that group's representative on the team which consisted of Bill Maynard, Dick Dyksterhuis, Bob Hamilton, Art Kono, Jim Page, and Ricky Malone. The team continued to work together with some later staff changes[33] through the development of the final Seattle Plan. Poc recalls the general climate in the administration during desegregation planning:

I think our biggest problem at that point was that it seemed as though Maynard did not have strong direction from the superintendent. Their philosophies about desegregation were different. I think that the administrators throughout the central office were struggling to find themselves. There was a lot of paranoia going on about

Moberly being a "hatchet man."³⁴ As a result people were more or less covering their tracks and were unwilling to stick their necks out or go that extra mile. It was difficult to get the administration to talk about desegregation which they didn't see happening immediately. They didn't want any more disruption in the schools. They didn't want any more irate calls from parents.

Partly it was that the superintendent was new. People didn't know him and therefore didn't trust him. And Maynard was gone a lot to conferences and meetings. Fortunately, Dyksterhuis and Maynard found a way to work together which worked out very well indeed. They understood each other. Their philosophies are not the same, but they complemented one another. Dyksterhuis had the technical expertise to put a sound plan together; Maynard had the charisma to sell it.³⁵

The school district was not geared up to attempt an aggressive desegregation effort in early 1977; simultaneously the community, in the form of racial minority and civil rights organizations, was becoming increasingly impatient with the lack of desegregation progress. Much of the pressure to increase desegregation efforts was coming from individuals and organizations which participated on the District-Wide Advisory Committee on Desegregation.

CHAPTER 3

JUST, RIGHT AND EQUITABLE

The Seattle School District has a long history of stating that it wants community involvement in public education. Sometimes community involvement even takes place. Regarding desegregation in Seattle, community members were genuinely involved in the decisions which were made, and the primary and official avenue for that involvement was the District-Wide Advisory Committee on Desegregation (DWAC).

DWAC was created as an advisory committee to Superintendent Loren Troxel in late 1974. Troxel had risen through the ranks of the district, unlike Bottomly and Moberly, who were hired from out-of-state. No substantial progress was made in desegregation during Troxel's tenure as superintendent.

Prior to 1975 two citizens' groups had been working cooperatively with the administration to assist with desegregation efforts. One was a nonprofit corporation, the Coalition for Quality Integrated Education, which had incorporated in 1971, bringing together three *ad hoc* groups which had formed to support middle school desegregation efforts. CQIE was the recipient of funds through the Emergency School Aid Act, Title VII, to assist the district with desegregation activities.

The second group was the Voluntary Racial Transfer Steering Committee. This body, which included many CQIE members, had also been created during the implementation of the Middle School Plan. It was re-formed each year to work with the administration and community to recruit voluntary racial transfer students both for the citywide voluntary racial transfer (VRT) program, and for the voluntary recruitment phase of the middle school assignments made each year, prior to the selection of students for mandatory assignment. Students had an opportunity to volunteer to transfer; then, when insufficient numbers were recruited, a random mandatory selection was made by computer to guarantee that middle schools were racially balanced.

Though other community groups in Seattle also had a commitment to desegregation, these two invested efforts on a week-by-week basis during most of each school year between 1971 and 1975 to attempt to bring about as much desegregation as possible.

On June 12, 1974, the Seattle School Board passed a resolution on desegregation, Resolution 1974–14. The resoution was one of the ones which Board member Patt Sutton describes as having been drafted by school district legal counsel Gary Little "to keep the wolf, in the form of civil rights groups in Seattle, from the door."

BE IT RESOLVED THAT:

1. Garfield High School shall be desegregated with the beginning of the 1975–76 school year. Desegregation shall be accomplished by the elimination of all transfers granted to students who would normally graduate from high school after June, 1975, who are not participating in the Voluntary Racial Transfer Program, and who are residents of the Garfield attendance area; by adjusting the Garfield attendance area boundaries; and by the development at Garfield of exemplary academic and occupational programs designed to attract students from the entire district.

2. The district shall commit and allocate resources to other multi-ethnic and multi-cultural secondary schools to maintain and enhance their drawing power and academic excellence.

3. Every school that is de facto segregated shall, during the 1974–75 school year, be paired with a school without a significant minority enrollment.

The paired schools will develop frequent informal contacts between the two staffs, student bodies and parent groups. Planning for the 1975–76 school year shall include multi-ethnic and multi-cultural exchanges involving teachers, students and families, shared educational experiences such as assemblies, field trips and short-term and long-term student transfers.

4. The district shall initiate immediately a boundary realignment study for those schools that are de facto segregated to determine the effect on the racial composition of school attendance areas of redrawing boundaries for 1975–76 with a conscious attempt to bring about a better ethnic balance.

5. The district's commitment to the Voluntary Transfer Program is reaffirmed. Support will be provided to make it of maximum effectiveness.

6. The administration is directed to provide and integrate resources to carry out the concepts and recommendations in the administrative reports including attention to facilities consolidation and upgrading, planning,

transportation patterns, multi-ethnic staffing, staff preparation, student assignment, transfer policies and placement procedures, necessary funding, community involvements, etc. An operational plan incorporating these elements is to be presented for Board consideration and subsequent approval by September 1, 1974.

The resolution committed the district to some specific actions to reaffirm a commitment to quality, integrated education. The district did not follow up on many of the provisions in the resolution, and Ann Siqueland, then director of CQIE, wrote a report, using the resolution and similar documents on desegregation in the district, to point out the numerous issues which the district had promised to address, but was not addressing. Because the voluntary racial transfer program was the primary desegregation plan in operation, the CQIE report mainly pointed out the lack of commitment to this program.

Board member Don Olson agreed that the district had not aggressively pursued its commitment to desegregate Seattle Public Schools through voluntary means, and Olson was interested in changing this.

As a strategy for making some progress in desegregation, the idea of a citizens' advisory committee in desegregation was proposed by Board member Don Olson, CQIE, and the district administration. The original committee was to include an umbrella group, which became the District-Wide Advisory Committee on Desegregation, and several subcommittees, including the Voluntary Racial Transfer (VRT) Steering Committee and the district's Title VII Advisory Committee, the body mandated by guidelines under which the district received desegregation funds from the Emergency School Aid Act, Title VII. In addition to members from the VRT Steering Commmittee and the Title VII Advisory Committee, DWAC's members were recruited from an extensive list of education-related, ethnic, and community organizations in Seattle. At least sixty organizations were invited to send representatives. CQIE's staff, along with the district's administration, drew up the list of organizations to be invited to join DWAC. Though the invitation list was long, not all organizations appointed members to serve on DWAC. The NAACP, CQIE, ACLU, Church Council of Greater Seattle, Parent-Teacher-Student Association (PTSA), Central Area School Council, and League of Women Voters were actively represented. At the May 28, 1975, meeting of DWAC, twenty-seven individuals representing organizations had been present, an additional twenty individuals representing other groups were listed as absent, six organizations who had not yet appointed representatives were also listed. DWAC's membership included representatives from community councils, school advisory groups, and citywide community organizations. The Seattle Chamber of Commerce, Municipal League and city government were not represented.

Dan Levant[1] was elected the first chairperson of DWAC, and Arlene Oki the first vice-chairperson. DWAC's charter was dated October 22, 1974, but was revised by DWAC members in August, 1975, to expand its responsibilities to include advising the School Board as well as Superintendent Troxel. Following this change DWAC's chair, Dan Levant, made numerous appearances before the School Board, which did not please Troxel. As Levant remembers:

I felt strongly that we could only be effective acting upon the School Board, and this immediately incurred the wrath of Superintendent Troxel. We went to the School Board and made statements intended to drive a wedge between the Board and the administration, and he was naturally very unhappy about it. We went through one period of about two months when he referred to me first as "Dan," then as "Mr. Levant," and then, at one meeting, as "that man." That was an index of how well we were doing. We were there to fight the administration. We were blasting the school district out of its comfort zone, into a very uncomfortable area. The intention was to make the school district do something it didn't want to do, and you could only do that by making it too uncomfortable for the district to stay where it was.[2]

DWAC's strategy during Levant's tenure as chair was to confront the school district on the issue of desegregation to produce some action. Neither Levant nor DWAC had a specific desegregation plan to suggest; rather, the group was hoping to disrupt the status quo and make the district look at the problems it had.

In the early period of DWAC's history, the committee established the Committee for Southeast Seattle Schools in an attempt to focus attention on this area — to broaden the understanding of the need for desegregation efforts, which previously had only addressed the central area of Seattle. According to Levant:

It was quite clear to some of us that the central area had made enormous progress and was no longer the focus of race problems in Seattle. The focus was becoming southeast Seattle, where the schools were becoming segregated quickly, where leadership was not present, where there was little community organization, and where there was no one to stand up to the School Board. What was needed was a political organization in southeast Seattle to do something about the feeling of helplessness.[3]

During 1975 and 1976, DWAC met regularly and selected one issue after another to bring to the attention of the School Board, demonstrating the district's lack of commitment to desegregation. The commitee's efforts did not cause much action on the part of the district, but the committee did provide a base on which several individuals representing several organizations could begin to construct a framework of ideas within which a unified community approach to desegregation could be developed. Communication links were established between representatives of such organizations as the NAACP, the League of Women Voters, the Central Area School Council, the Church Council of Greater Seattle, the Committee for Southeast Seattle Schools, PTSA, and the like. By January 1977, several of the organizations with representation on DWAC had identified most of the issues which would become objectified in the desegregation "criteria" DWAC formalized in February 1977, which became the basis for the School Board's desegregation criteria, which in turn determined the kind of plan Seattle would adopt.

The consensus developed by the dialogue which took place through DWAC is revealed in the similarity of statements made to the School Board on desegregation in December 1976 and January 1977, including statements from the League of Women Voters, the NAACP, the Church Council of Greater Seattle, the Central Area School Council, and the Committee for Southeast Seattle Schools, as well as DWAC. It was also during 1976 that the ACLU and NAACP made a decision to support desegregation efforts in Seattle, leading to the threat of a lawsuit.

DWAC was a small group of deeply committed individuals, probably not representing a cross-section of opinions in Seattle. Some members of DWAC served on the committee from its inception to the adoption of the Seattle Plan. Arlene Oki, Constance Herring and Kay Groves are three of these individuals. For them, membership in DWAC was more than a four-year commitment of long hours and regular meetings. Herring represented the NAACP, and Oki, a member of numerous community groups, brought the perspective of the Asian community continually before DWAC. Groves served as president of Seattle PTSA Council from 1976 to 1978.

When David Moberly was hired as the superintendent of Seattle Public Schools in the summer of 1976, Dan Levant forced the new superintendent to meet with him privately for half an hour. The meeting was a cold one, with Moberly giving the impression that he had more important things to do than discuss desegregation with the chair of the district's advisory committee. Recalling their meeting, Levant says:

> Moberly made a couple of trips to Seattle before he started to work here, and an invitation went out for him to meet with representatives of school and community groups. I requested a personal audience with Moberly. My intention was to impress upon him that there was pressure to make desegregation a high priority. When I was told that I could not have a personal appointment, I said that I would make that known publicly, and I was granted thirty minutes with Dr. Moberly, privately. I would call it a cold meeting, polite but very cold. Moberly was hired to straighten out an administrative mess. While he was aware of the pressure to desegregate, he had no intention of making that an immediate priority. He didn't like what I was saying. Nothing much was accomplished. That's how we started – cold. And it went downhill from there.[4]

There was no love lost between David Moberly and Dan Levant. The two probably could not have developed the candid working relationship that did develop between Levant's successor, Richard Andrews, and the superintendent.

When William Maynard was appointed director of a new desegregation office in August 1976, he and Dan Levant worked well together for a while, but that relationship soon deteriorated also. As Levant recalls:

> I think Maynard took the job with the idea of accomplishing something with desegregation, but I think he soon realized that Moberly did not want to proceed very quickly. I think Maynard thought he could handle Moberly and could maneuver Moberly into a position where he would have no choice except to proceed. But Maynard could not handle it. I don't know precisely what went on between Moberly and Maynard, but I know there was showdown after showdown. The superintendent had an agenda that nobody else knew, and it was clear to me that he was going to call the shots.[5]

Levant began to believe that Maynard was not going to be able to do anything substantial with desegregation, though he may have personally wanted to. There was an obvious disparity between what the School Board had authorized Maynard to do in desegregation planning, and what Moberly had told Maynard to do. This difference was brought out at the January 3 meeting to which DWAC invited the School Board to clarify what the parameters were for desegregation planning (see Don Olson's report on page 27).

The superintendent's decision to develop only voluntary desegregation methods for the 1977–78 school year precipitated Dan Levant's resignation as chairperson of DWAC. This move was motivated both by personal considerations and by a desire to focus negative attention on the Magnet Plan.

I was elected for a year and had no intention of continuing permanently as chair of DWAC. I was starting my own business, and I was exhausted. There did not appear to be anybody who could take over the chair, and the situation was very intense.

When the announcement of the magnet program was made, I can't say I was surprised, but I was furious. This all came out of Moberly's head and had nothing to do with the public process.

The immediate response was a statement from the NAACP that they would fight the school district, that they were locked into a position which would include going to court if necessary.

I had threatened to quit a few months earlier. A public resignation is a very powerful political statement, and since I had to get out of that position anyway, it was a question of how best to use the resignation. It was one of those cold, calculated acts, except that it was done in great heat after about twenty-four hours of heavy thinking. I was outraged by the brutality of the superintendent imposing the Magnet Plan in defiance of everybody else who was working on desegregation.

The Magnet Plan had been put together too hastily; there had been no preparation, no groundwork. I thought of the Magnet Plan as a sitting duck: the quicker I could attack it, while it was still on the ground, before it took off, the better. It would soon build up momentum, and I thought I had about forty-eight hours to take the best shot I could, so that by the time the plan got to the Board and went public, it would be on the defensive. I resigned that night. I sometimes think the major contribution that I made to the whole process was wounding the Magnet Plan at the beginning.

The original plans were for white programs and black programs, academic programs and vocational programs. It was racist. But the real danger of the magnet program was that it would tie up the district for the next three to five years. It would be another five years before we could get back to the point of saying, "Well, this hasn't worked. What do we do now?"[6]

Levant helped create a negative image of the Magnet Plan in some people's minds, which continued through the adoption of the Seattle Plan.

Levant had also expected that the rest of DWAC might resign, and the committee seriously considered doing that. Levant felt that because the superintendent had inherited DWAC and had no ties to the committee, he would never listen to it. After resigning, Levant became active in the ACLU's efforts to force desegregation by threatening to file a lawsuit. Levant was concerned that the pressure of a lawsuit not come only from the black community, because that could create a black/white conflict in Seattle.

DWAC members did not resign, and the committee was able to recruit a new chair, who also understood the need for the superintendent to feel some "ownership" of the advisory committee. Levant was somewhat surprised at the turn of events when Dr. Richard Andrews became the chair of DWAC.

I wasn't aware of anybody who I thought could handle the situation at that time. I guess I thought I was indispensable. As it turned out, I wasn't, because Dick Andrews, to my surprise (because initially I didn't think he could do it), turned DWAC around. Dick Andrews is a political creature and he has enormous energy. He managed to do what I thought had to be done, without allowing the superintendent off the hook. I think Dick did a beautiful job. It was perfect.[7]

Dan Levant and Dick Andrews are different personalities. Levant describes himself as a Saul Alinski type of activist. He and his wife Sara moved to Seattle from New York City in 1967, initially to the suburban community of Bellevue, where the Levants were impressed with the openness of community involvement in decision-making. They began participating in community meetings "for inexpensive entertainment," attempting to persuade the Bellevue School Board to adopt a voluntary desegregation program. Moving to the multiracial Madrona area in Seattle, they participated in efforts in the central area to improve the quality of public education there. Levant served on the Central Area School Council for four years. Many of his ideas about ways to promote change in the public schools — including the belief that it was necessary to work with the School Board (policy-makers) rather than the administration — were developed through his experiences in central area school politics, his confrontation style, and his belief that for changes to take place in a minority impacted area of the city, leadership must come from minority individuals, but must also include the participation of members of the white community.

In looking for a new chairperson, DWAC sought a black and approached Jerome Page, executive director of the Seattle Urban League.[8] The Urban League's education committee was chaired at that time by Richard Andrews, a professor of educational administration at the University of Washington. Andrews is not black, although his Afro hair style and multiracial adopted family have left many with that impression. Andrews was raised on a farm in Indiana and came to the Seattle area in 1968 to take a teaching position in the

Educational Administration Department at the University after earning a Ph.D. at Purdue University. He had been active in public school issues, primarily as an advocate for alternative schools. Though he favored desegregation, he did not have extensive experience with past efforts.

Andrews had just finished leading a fight to prevent the school district from closing University Heights Elementary School, the site of an alternative program he had helped begin. This fight included a suit filed against the district, which the alternative-advocate parents technically won because the district had not filed an environmental impact statement. The parents were in the process of raising money to pay off legal costs, and Andrews was looking forward to a rest, with nothing but fund-raising bake sales to worry about, when Jerome Page asked him to serve as the chair of DWAC:

Jerry Page asked me if I would be willing to chair DWAC. I really wasn't interested. I had just gone through a major confrontation with the district. The first person I talked to was Barbara [Andrews]. If Barbara had said, "No," I would not have done it, but she said, "It's something we feel strongly committed about and it obviously needs to be done."

I then called three members of the administration and I said that I had been approached to chair DWAC, and I wanted their assessment. Were they really interested in a community involvement model for bringing about desegregation? If they weren't, I wouldn't touch it with a ten-foot pole, because I was not interested in getting back into an adversary role. They said they wanted community involvement.

Next I went to the DWAC meeting. I understood the active participation was down to about six people before that night and those six sat around and commiserated. That night at least forty members of the committee were present. For the most part, they were people that had been involved for a long time.

I told them they would have to put themselves into a study posture. I really hit them hard on why they were opposed to magnets, and I was utterly amazed at their total nondefensiveness.

I was so impressed that I said, "Yes," right on the spot. And I said, "Okay, I want a committee to do this, this and this, and I want volunteers." I got them.[9]

DWAC's first effort after Richard Andrews took over as the chair was to develop criteria which they would use to judge any desegregation plan. Andrews recalls:

I called a Steering Committee together and we had our first chance to develop criteria to judge a desegregation plan, and within a week we had that done. The Steering

Committee identified nine criteria, and the full committee added four more. I wrote the rationale for each one of the criteria out of the literature on desegregation. That night over fifty people came to the meeting to deal with the criteria. I marched them through those thirteen criteria by parliamentary procedures. I said, "We're not leaving here tonight until we have the criteria."

I really believe that the committee's thirteen-point criteria is what predetermined what happened thereafter. Many community organizations endorsed the criteria.[10]

Andrews's leadership allowed DWAC to formulate the ideas it had been developing as objective criteria. The fact that many organizations easily endorsed the criteria demonstrated the consensus on desegregation which had been developed during the two previous years of discussion.

The early weeks of Andrews's tenure as chairperson of DWAC were intensively active ones, a preview of the quantity of work DWAC was to complete while the Seattle Plan was being devised. Remembering this time, Andrews says:

I took over the committee on February 7 [1977]. The criteria were complete two weeks later. At our next meeting Bill Maynard presented the Magnet Plan. I couldn't believe that it was a four-page document. I expected to see a full-blown plan. It listed the schools and the program options, and it summarized briefly a bit of the data they had gathered in a survey of the community.

Bill was saying that citizens cannot be involved in the planning function, and he said, for example, "Do you want to go through the 235,000 pages of computer printouts on the survey?"[11] I said, "When will the copy be available and where?" We got the printout and went over to the Seattle Teachers Association building. We started going through the data, collecting information around our thirteen criteria. And we slaved.[12]

Using the computer printout (fewer than 235,000 pages), DWAC conducted an analysis to determine if the Magnet Plan would successfully desegregate schools and if the plan met the requirements of their new criteria, and wrote a 72-page analysis of the district's 4-page Magnet Desegregation Plan. The report was written in less than two weeks. On March 7 the School Board was scheduled to vote on adoption of the Magnet Plan. DWAC delivered its 72-page analysis to the School Board that day. The Board did not ask one question about the report.

While some DWAC members were analyzing computer data, others were in Houston and Dallas observing magnet schools in operation. A multiracial group from DWAC attended a magnet school conference there along with some school personnel. The results of the analysis of the computer data, and the firsthand observations of magnet schools by DWAC members produced the same conclusions. Magnets would not work on an elementary level because they created in-building segregation. On a high school level, where substantial funding was available, magnets were educationally successful and exciting but produced few student transfers. There was no way to guarantee desegregation with magnet programs because a mandatory backup to a specialized program was not practical.

Through all of the hard work DWAC was undertaking, Andrews was attempting to convince the district of the high quality of expertise which existed within DWAC.

The thing the district didn't understand was that DWAC was made up of essentially graduate students or people with degrees, people who have all the skills that the administration had and, in many cases, were better. The district's perception was that citizens are a bunch of little old ladies in tennis shoes, housewives who have spent most of their time at home and are deeply emotionally tied to their own children. They had never stopped to analyze the general, professional level of the membership of DWAC. Almost everyone on the committee is a professional person of some kind.[13]

Andrews's characterization of the district's perception of DWAC's membership revealed several facts: Much of DWAC's membership was female, and virtually all were parents of children in the public schools. Many were college-educated and many held down full-time jobs while particpating on DWAC. Connie Herring, the NAACP's representative, was in bank management; Arlene Oki, a registered nurse, was working in a local hospital; Annie Jones, representing the Central Area School Council, was a consumer affairs advocate for the Central Area Motivation Program; Sam Shoji, representing the Japanese American Citizens' League (JACL) was employed by the Veteran's Administration; Jerry Skutt, the representative from the Municipal League, was then director of the Central Puget Sound Economic Development District; Patte Poc, a PTSA representative, was a theater production person; Judith Youngman, representing the Wallingford Community Council, was a bank teller; Dean Lydle was an engineering professor at the University of Washington; Grover Haynes was a manufacturing engineer at the Boeing Company, and Hilo Hasagawa was a Seattle teacher.

Some of DWAC's members were staff members of the organizations they represented: Cheryl Crawford was the education director of the Urban League; Reese Lindquist was on the staff of the Seattle Teachers Association; Arlis Stewart was the director of the People Power Coalition; Sidney Freeman was the City of Seattle school liaison; Ann Siqueland was the desegregation project director for the Church Council of Greater Seattle; Rob Makin was on the staff of the Chamber of Commerce; and Jonis Davis and Barbara Cook were on the staff of the American Friends Service Committee. Other organizational representatives included the League of Women Voters (Ellen Zarter), Seattle Council PTSA (Kay Groves and Susan Wallace), and CQIE (Nadine Patti). Kathy Elskie, one of DWAC's vice-presidents, represented the Ballard Area Consortium; Fabiola Woods represented the compensatory education parents; and Carol Richman represented the Madrona Community Council. Others were individual members — Jan Kumasaka, Barbara Beuschlein and Mary Ann Goe — but had extensive experience working with the public schools. Sixty-one people were serving on DWAC on June 24, 1977.

Despite the high level of expertise on DWAC, when the School Board adopted the Magnet Plan, contrary to the DWAC analysis, Dick Andrews was prepared to disband the committee. Moberly had called it a special-interest group, and no one on the School Board had a positive thing to say about it. The superintendent and School Board were locked into attempting to desegregate the district with a voluntary student transfer strategy, and given that fact, Bill Maynard had an impossible job to perform. The superintendent was not supporting Maynard's efforts to desegregate, and Maynard, probably in part to express his disagreement with the superintendent, produced a sketchy four-page desegregation plan. It was necessary to persuade the superintendent to feel some commitment to DWAC in order for the committee to be effective. Andrews recommended to DWAC's Steering Committee that they recommend to the superintendent that DWAC be disbanded. The committee agreed, and Andrews carried that recommendation to the superintendent.

Moberly was surprised by the move. DWAC wanted the superintendent to appoint the chair of a new committee as well as its membership. The superintendent agreed.

An interim committee was appointed in April, composed of all of the old DWAC members except one member of the press. Representatives from the

Municipal League, the Chamber of Commerce, and the City of Seattle were added to address the perception that DWAC was a special-interest group. Letters were sent out by the district to between sixty and a hundred community organizations, inviting them to send representatives to DWAC. Community organizations reappointed their old representatives, and a few additional organizations chose to be represented. On June 15, Andrews received a letter from the superintendent appointing him as the chair of DWAC. Whether the superintendent could politically have done anything else but reappoint Andrews is doubtful. But, in addition, the superintendent and Andrews had developed a working relationship during the spring of 1977 which continued through the adoption of the Seattle Plan. As a university professor, Andrews had credentials which impressed Moberly, and it was soon clear that DWAC would report directly to the superintendent, and would not embarrass him publicly by going over his head to the School Board. DWAC rewrote its bylaws reversing the change that Dan Levant had made in August 1975, and judiciously avoided ever making statements to the School Board publicly unless invited to do so by the superintendent. This did not prevent informal contacts with School Board members, which were numerous. Nor did it prevent DWAC members, who were the spokespeople for various community organizations, from speaking to the School Board on behalf of their respective organizations. DWAC's new approach was effective. By working with the administration to develop the plan, rather than reacting to a plan, the group had a voice in the development of the desegregation plan. Andrews succeeded in gaining virtually everyone's respect for his professionalism and hard work with DWAC, the administration, and the community. His litany was that Seattle would desegregate with a plan that was "just, right and equitable."

DWAC's members had been working within the various community organizations they represented to develop support for desegregation beginning with the establishment of the advisory committee in 1975. This continued through 1977. Seattle could not have desegregated without a court order if it had not been for this extensive activity on the part of a variety of community organizations. This activity was the result, in part, of energy generated by discussions at DWAC.

A look at the activities of numerous community groups prior to and during the spring of 1977 is necessary to see the total picture of community involvement which brought about the Seattle Plan.

CHAPTER 4

NASAKE GA NAI

What the 1954 *Brown* decision means to blacks interested in equal opportunity in public education, the January 1974 *Lau* v. *Nichol* Supreme Court decision on bilingual education means to the Asian American and Hispanic communities in the country. The issues in the two Supreme Court decisions are different, but the intent of both is to provide equal opportunity in public education guaranteed by the Fourteenth Amendment. The *Lau* case, brought on behalf of non-English-speaking Chinese students in San Francisco, resulted in a decision that public school systems must provide appropriate instruction to students who do not speak English proficiently:

It seems obvious that the Chinese-speaking minority receives fewer benefits than [others under] a system which denies them a meaningful opportunity to participate in the educational program – all earmarks of discrimination banned by the regulations . . . .

Where inability to speak and understand the English language excludes national origin–minority group children from effective participation in the educational program offered by a school district, the district must take affirmative steps to rectify the language deficiency in order to open its instructional program to these students.[1]

The Supreme Court did not define how non-English-speaking students should be served, suggesting that two possibilities would be instruction in the student's native language and English language proficiency classes. The U.S. Department of Health, Education and Welfare was given the responsibility of developing "*Lau* compliance standards."

In 1975, Seattle Public Schools were found out of compliance in some of the areas of civil rights assurances the district had signed to receive funds through the Emergency School Aid Act (Title VII); service to bilingual

54 *Without a Court Order*

students was one area. Federal funds were withheld for a time, and the district lost in a challenge of the noncompliance ruling.

The relationship between the desegregation of the student body in Seattle Public Schools and the requirement that Seattle provide appropriate instruction to non-English-speaking students, caused an uneasy undercurrent while the desegregation plan was being developed in Seattle. The question of whether non-English-speaking students would be counted as "minority" students and participate in the desegregation plan had to be addressed. In San Francisco, recent Asian immigrants in need of bilingual services were not included in desegregation efforts. The largest number of non-English-speaking immigrant students attending Seattle Public Schools were (and still are) Asian — mainly Chinese, Filipino and Southeast Asian.

The primary vehicle for community involvement in the issue of service to bilingual students in Seattle is the district's Bilingual Advisory Commission. The chair of the commission in 1977 was John Huston, an Episcopal priest, who coordinates the Washington Association of Churches' Southeast Asian resettlement program.

No one from the district's Bilingual Advisory Commission actively participated on DWAC, but the commission members were kept informed on desegregation planning by John Huston and commission member Don Kazama, who were involved in the Church Council of Greater Seattle's desegregation efforts. The commission did discuss whether or not it wished to advise the district to exclude non-English-speaking students from the desegregation plan. Ultimately the commission chose not to make that recommendation, but instead encouraged the district to guarantee that students in need of bilingual services would still receive them under the proposed desegregation plan. If non-English-speaking students were excluded from the Seattle Plan, the burden of student transfers would fall much more heavily on English-speaking Asian students, probably creating hard feelings between recent immigrants and second-, third-, and fourth-generation Asian Americans.

When adopted, the Seattle Plan counted non-English-speaking minority students as a part of the "minority" count in schools needing to be desegregated. Don Kazama, a retired social worker and member of the Bilingual Advisory Commission, discusses bilingual education and desegregation:

Most members of the advisory commission emotionally were in favor of excluding bilingual students from desegregation. It was much stronger at the building level. I argued for their inclusion. We were discussing mainstreaming bilingual students, which meant they had to participate in the desegregation plan. I also did not want to create any hard feelings between black and Asian kids or their parents. I did not want hostility developing; it was already there to a certain extent because previous desegregation had involved mainly black students — almost ninety percent were black.

By and large the Asian community attitude was that if they ignored desegregation, it might go away. And I would say parents were fearful.[2]

Historically, public school desegregation has not seemed as significant a civil rights issue to the Asian American community in Seattle as it has to the black community. Few cities in the country have desegregated a population which includes Asian students. In some parts of the country, Asians have been defined as "white" during recent past history. These facts provided the basis for some possible conflict between the black and Asian communities in Seattle. Past desegregation efforts in Seattle had only addressed the predominantly black schools in the central area, ignoring the multiracial schools in the southeast part of the city.

The U.S. Department of Health, Education and Welfare includes in its definition of "minority" blacks, Asian Americans, Hispanics and Native Americans. While Seattle's Hispanic and Native American populations did not reside in large numbers in any particular geographic area, and no school could be considered "segregated" solely because of its percentage of either of these two ethnic groups, the large numbers of Asian students in Seattle schools would clearly be involved in any desegregation plan. The Asian community, therefore, needed to be involved in desegregation planning for Seattle.

Arlene Oki was undoubtedly the most active Asian American involved in desegregation planning. She joined DWAC at the beginning as a representative of the district's Title VII Advisory Committee. Oki was also a board member of the Coalition for Quality Integrated Education, a member of the Church Council Task Force on Racial Justice and a member of the Committee for Southeast Seattle Schools. She served as a vice-president of DWAC.

Oki effectively communicated the concerns of the Asian community wherever she was involved, and attempted to encourage other Asians to participate in the decisions which were being made:

As desegregation discussions began to develop, I could see the need for more Asian involvement. It is hard for white liberals to advocate for Asians. Somehow most don't feel that Asians are in dire need; or they feel that where discrimination is blatant, it isn't against Asians — it is against blacks.

The Asian community was kept informed about what was happening through the Committee for Southeast Seattle Schools. And Sam Shoji was an effective liaison with the Japanese American Citizens' League. He reported back every month once he got on DWAC. Other than CQIE's newspaper, *In Touch,* and school district literature, there were no formal means of communications with the Asian community.

A lot of organizations were invited to send representatives to DWAC, and those representatives never came.

The Church Council made an attempt to reach the Asian community. I did go before a couple of Asian groups — the Filipino Teachers Association and the Asian American Educators Association — and talked about desegregation planning. Some of the staff of CQIE tried to inform Asian parents about the issues and encourage them to get involved.

I felt that the Asians on DWAC were not truly representative of the Asian community; we represented only our own ideas, but always with a concern for the educational futures of Asian children in mind. We knew some form of desegregation was inevitable, and it was our mission to make sure the plan reflected the delicate and special mix of all the children who reside in Seattle.

It was feared that a court-ordered desegregation plan would result in the dispersal of Asian students to a degree that a greater potential for loss of ethnic identity would exist; that our students would be better off in the reassignment plan if they were allowed to go together in sufficient numbers.

We talked with people in the community, but our sphere of influence on this controversial issue was very small.

Historically, Asians have not felt they had anything to gain from desegregation. If anything, Asians were perceived as a group who might possibly oppose a desegregation plan.[3]

Oki recalls the activities of DWAC during Dan Levant's tenure as chair of the advisory group:

A lot of us had come to the conclusion that a mandatory plan was the only way to accomplish our goal of integrating schools in this district. There were, however, differences of opinion about a definition of racial imbalance. We hassled over that a lot. Some of us felt that the definition should allow more minority students in schools and others felt that we should adhere to the HEW guideline[4] of fifty percent total minority.

The committee [DWAC] felt that it had been misled in terms of the kind of commitment the district would make to the voluntary racial transfer program.[5] Dan Levant was the most outspoken person. Although we were essentially a superintendent's committee, he had no qualms about going to the press. He got advice from Charles Royer on how to approach the press.[6] The only way Dan was going to move the district was by publicizing the problems that the committee was having. Dan Levant happened to be the right person at the right time, moving us close to what we wanted to achieve.

And the committee did not like magnets. I have never liked the Magnet Plan for a number of reasons, primarily because it offers unequal educational opportunities. After the Magnet Plan was adopted, it did not help the school district to achieve the degree of desegregation that we felt it should have. We knew then we would have to seek a mandatory assignment plan.[7]

Individual Asian Americans who were active in efforts which resulted in the adoption of the Seattle Plan were, like Oki, almost exclusively Nisei (second-generation Japanese Americans), and the two organizations which were most active were the Japanese American Citizens' League (JACL) and the Asian American Education Association (AAEA), the latter including representatives from all Asian groups.

Sam Shoji represented JACL on DWAC from January 1977 on. Shoji, a resident of southeast Seattle, is a Nisei. He joined DWAC after Arlene Oki made a plea for greater involvement by Asian community people at a meeting of the Seattle chapter of JACL. As Shoji recalls:

My involvement in school issues and the problems of desegregation and minority concerns dates back to 1969–70. I was then a member of the Cleveland High School Area Advisory Committee.[8] We recognized that some form of equitable distribution of populations and quality education programs within the schools needed to be addressed.

When Dan Levant was the chair of DWAC, just prior to his resignation, Arlene Oki came to a meeting of JACL to make a report, and said that JACL needed to have a direct voice on DWAC because of the effect desegregation was going to have on the Asian community. She wanted someone else from JACL to become active, rather than just have her report regularly. I said, "Okay, if you need help. I'll give you a hand."

Asians, at least Japanese Americans, living here in the United States tend to take a pretty passive role. It's been a learned process, not a cultural process, a way of fitting into the American society when the majority population is more powerful. There is also quite a bit of respect and authority given to educators, which includes the educators who make decisions within the educational system. There is also the feeling of *nasake ga nai*, which means, "It's going to happen anyway, it's too bad, but it's inevitable, so why fight it?"[9]

The Japanese American Citizens' League in Seattle has about eight hundred members, many of whom live outside the boundaries of the city of Seattle. Emigration of Japanese Americans to the suburbs of Seattle takes place at approximately the same rate as the emigration of whites. The Seattle chapter of JACL is one of the most active of the almost one hundred chapters in the country. In many rural areas of the country, JACL chapters are primarily social organizations. In Seattle, the group has actively pursued social and political issues.

The history of Japanese Americans and other Asian groups in Seattle and on the West Coast includes many experiences with discrimination, one of the most tragic of which was the incarceration of Japanese Americans during World War II. In 1942, President Roosevelt signed Executive Order 9066, which placed all Japanese Americans in relocation camps "for national security reasons." Two-thirds of the individuals relocated were American citizens, and virtually all Japanese Americans currently living in Seattle were either incarcerated themselves or had family members who were. The Seattle chapter of JACL has led a battle to gain reparations from the U.S. Government for the loss of property which resulted from the relocation.

At the same time, according to Sam Shoji, there is still the knowledge that if discrimination is practiced in this country in any form against any group, all minority groups are vulnerable. As he puts it:

When people holler about sending the blacks back to Africa, you have to ask who are they going to try and get next? It's not going to stop. I thought that working for desegregation would be a way to help.[10]

In March 1977, Sam Shoji was part of a delegation from DWAC which traveled to Dallas to a conference on magnet schools and observed magnet programs in operation. The School Board was scheduled to adopt a voluntary student transfer magnet plan that month. Shoji recalls:

I went to Dallas to the first annual conference on magnet schools. In Dallas they had really financed some magnets, such as flying in artists[11] from various portions of the country to teach creative arts. This attracted many students to participate in voluntary desegregation.[12]

With enough money, magnets could be exciting, but Seattle didn't have that money. Magnets also raised the question of unequal allocation of resources to some students.

Hilo Hasegawa, a teacher in Seattle, was an active member of DWAC during the development of the Seattle Plan. Jan Kumasaka, a member of the Committee for Southeast Seattle Schools and CQIE, participated periodically. Both are Japanese American.

Gary Higashi, another Japanese American, was the president of Seattle's Asian American Education Association in 1976–77. A teacher in the Seattle Public Schools, Higashi had taught in desegregated Meany Middle School. He has lived both in predominately white West Seattle and the multiracial southeast area; his multiracial adopted children attend Seattle Public Schools. Higashi, who became a member of the Church Council's task force in the spring of 1977, was also a member of DWAC, though he did not participate frequently, and of JACL. He currently works for the State Superintendent of Public Instruction in the area of bilingual education.

By the spring of 1977, the NAACP and the ACLU were not the only community groups discussing threatening to sue the school district because of lack of movement to end segregation. As a representative from JACL, Higashi attended a meeting called in April 1977 by the Church Council of Greater Seattle to discuss the possibility of developing an expanded group of community organizations to join with the NAACP and the ACLU in a threatened suit to force desegregation. While JACL did not participate in the threatened suit, AAEA, with Higashi as president, did vote to be a plaintiff in a suit.

Higashi describes the experience of desegregation:

There is a very large number of middle-class Japanese Americans who see themselves as having attained success, and do not feel their education was hurt by being in schools which were predominately Asian. Instead, they look for a situation where there is a preponderance of Asian children because they feel that in that situation their traditional educational values will be expressed.

On the other side there was the larger question of opportunity for children in general, of children being isolated. There was also a desire to look at the common history of minority people. Once people begin to raise their sights a bit, they see the importance of involving themselves in the desegregation issue.

There were those people in the Japanese community who were supportive of desegregation and worked as individuals, such as Sam Shoji, Arlene Oki, and Don Kazama. But they were a leading edge, pulling people along with them. They were not typical. Part of their frustration has always been that they have been so far in the forefront that when they turn around to see who is following, there are not many people there. But Asians also do not have equal opportunity. The few who were active in desegregation efforts were speaking, in some instances, with the unspoken tongues of many who were silent.[13]

If desegregation in Seattle was to be brought about by court order, the possibility existed that a compromise plan might be worked out during the process of litigation. Plaintiffs who filed the lawsuit would be in a position to participate in the decision on a desegregation plan. It was important that the Asian community be represented in a coalition of groups bringing suit against the school district, in order that the concerns of that community be represented in a court decision.

The AAEA, a pan-Asian group, was prepared to serve in that role. The fact that the AAEA voted to sue the school district is an indication that some leadership in the Asian community in Seattle did want to help shape the future of public education in a desegregation plan.

AAEA was the logical Asian group to participate. Not only was it composed of educators, but included in its leadership were representatives of most Asian communities – Filipino, Chinese, Japanese, Korean and Samoan. It is probably misleading to suggest that an "Asian" community exists. There are probably more cultural and linguistic differences between Japanese, Chinese, Filipino, Samoan, Korean, Vietnamese, and other Asian peoples than between German, Irish, Italian, French and English. Though racially an Asian, like a Caucasian, group can be identified, cultural differences often keep Asian groups of different national origin apart in their approaches to issues in public education and elsewhere. For this reason, the AAEA's willingness to join in litigation is important.

Gary Higashi remembers:

I became AAEA's president in 1976, and within the organization there were discussions about why the district isn't moving toward desegregation. We began to have some forums discussing desegregation, and there was some interest in the magnet program.

The threat of a lawsuit was coming from the NAACP, ACLU, and the Church Council, and the discussions within AAEA were about how this would effect Asian children.

Asians began to see the importance of really involving themselves with desegregation, and as an organization we took a look at desegregation efforts.

Our concern was that the plan be mandatory. That was absolutely essential. If it was voluntary, the net effect would be that there would be little movement from students of any race under the guise of freedom of choice. We were unanimous in our feelings about that as an organization.

The decision to participate in the lawsuit was basically the point of view that you had to have your ace in the hole. People don't act, unfortunately, unless you prod them to action by holding a club over their heads. That's why it made sense to be involved in this. The threat of the lawsuit is one of the major reasons that the Board adopted the Seattle Plan. If we hadn't talked about suing them, they would have put it off for two years or maybe wouldn't have done anything.[14]

CHAPTER 5

OUT OF THE MELTING POT INTO THE FIRE OF COURT ACTION

The AAEA agreed to participate in a lawsuit at the invitation of the Church Council of Greater Seattle. A look at the activities of the Church Council beginning in 1975 is necessary to understand why this invitation was extended.

The Church Council of Greater Seattle, which had historically supported desegregation efforts in Seattle, renewed its activity through involvement in the DWAC.

Don Daughtry, pastor of Beacon Avenue United Church of Christ, had been appointed to serve as the representative to DWAC by the Church Council in 1975. Daughtry, a white clergyman, had an active interest in school matters in the southeast area of Seattle where he lived, and through discussions of desegregation at DWAC, soon became convinced that the Church Council must become actively involved in the issue.

The transfer of minority teachers out of inner-city schools (central and southeast areas) required by HEW was of grave concern to Daughtry, who saw it as an application of the archaic "melting pot" philosophy. Daughtry's feelings were expressed in a sermon delivered to his congregation in the summer of 1976.

Seattle has felt the impact of the Department of Health, Education and Welfare's use of the past vision and its strategies for solving today's injustices. That vision of a melting pot society brought on the transfer of teachers in this manner: having 16 percent minority teachers in Seattle schools, HEW wanted the district to have 16 percent minority teachers in each school.... HEW got what it wanted. The imbalance of [sic] percentage of minority teachers and minority pupils was lost sight of and we heard few calls for a strong affirmative action program geared to raising the percentage of minority teachers to that of the pupils. Children in "minority impacted" schools . . . have been cheated of [sic] needed adult minority presence/leadership models.[1]

Instead of hiring additional minority teachers for schools in predominately white schools in the district, and thereby increasing the percentage of minority staff to approximate the percentage of minority students in the district, the school administration distributed the relatively small corps of minority teachers in Seattle equally to all schools.

At the end of the negotiations between the school district and HEW over the staff desegregation issue, HEW indicated it would be looking at the district's student-assignment policy. Should the federal government require the district to desegregate its student population in the same manner that the staff was desegregated, all schools could have a seventeen percent black population, a nine percent Asian population, and three percent each of Native American and Hispanic populations. A full citywide redistribution of racial minority students would result in those students being represented in very small numbers in each classroom, thereby diminishing the opportunity for maintaining ethnic and cultural identity. Citywide desegregation would also mean that the burden of student transfers would again be placed primarily on minority students, because most of the minority students attending schools in the central and southeast areas of the city would have to transfer out of these schools.

In January of 1976, the Church Council board of directors, at Daughtry's suggestion, established a Task Force on Racial Justice in Education. The task force was composed of equal numbers of black, Asian American and white members, with some representation from Native American and Chicano communities, clergy, lay people, women and men. Most of the task force members had a long history of involvement in civil rights or desegregation efforts. Several had ties to other organizations which were interested in public school desegregation. From March through October of 1976, the task force met regularly and discussed strategies to bring about racial justice in education without limiting itself to the subject of eliminating segregation. Dialogue involving task force members was also going on during this time in other community organizations. Daughtry, for example, who was cochairperson of the task force, was on the board of the Seattle PTSA Council. Arlene Oki, another member of the task force, was on the district's Title VII (Emergency School Aid Act) Advisory Committee, DWAC, the board of CQIE and the Committee for Southeast Seattle Schools. Tony Orange, then director of CQIE, was the recent past-president of CASC. Henrietta Mathews had worked in the district's desegregation office for many years, and her husband was a member of the Central Area Civil Rights Committee. Peter Jamero, cochairperson of the task force, was a recently unsuccessful candidate for the School Board with strong ties to organizations in the Filipino community. Phil Hayasaka was the recent past director of the Seattle Human Rights Commission. Jonathan Rhone, pastor of the Prim Tabernacle AME Church, was a member of the Black United Clergy for Action (BUCFA). Ann Siqueland was recent director of CQIE. Tony Ogilvie was on the staff of the State Superintendent of Public Instruction with responsibility for bilingual programs. Joan Stewart was a white central area parent. The Reverend Dr. William Cate, president/director of the Church Council, attended all of the task force meetings.

The discussions which took place from March to October of 1976 at meetings of the task force not only represented the ideas of its members, but also grew out of discussions that were simultaneously going on in other community organizations in the city. By October, task force members felt that they understood the issues concerning desegregation, which could be expressed in a pluralistic approach to public education, and that they could formulate a statement which would represent, as clearly as possible, a consensus of much of the city on the issue.

The statement went through several drafts during the month of November before the committee was satisfied with its content and wording. At that point, the statement was shown to other community organizations for comment. One specific meeting was organized by Cecil Murray, pastor of First AME Church and member of BUCFA, to which leaders from the black and Asian American communities were invited. Many of the Asian American clergy in the city were present, along with representatives from BUCFA, Walter Hubbard, representative of the Central Area Civil Rights Committee, and Dorothy Hollingsworth, the one black member on the Seattle School Board. As a result of the meeting, an addition to the original statement was written which listed each school that was segregated and noted the racial percentage that school would maintain at the end of the desegregation process.

After this review, the task force was ready to take its statement before the board of directors of the Church Council, which adopted the statement on December 14, 1976. Endorsements of the statement were then secured from several community organizations, numerous clergy members and several bishops with denominational offices in Seattle.

During the process of developing the statement on pluralism, Don Daughtry had met with denominational groups of clergy in Seattle, as well as with local church bishops. The offices of fifteen local denominational judicatories are located in Seattle, and these bishops met each Thursday morning for breakfast at the Synod Office of the Lutheran Church in America, providing an excellent opportunity for various community issues to be discussed with church leaders.

The statement began with the comment that the school district was facing the possibility of legal action[2] as the result of its "lack of compliance in desegregating its schools," and said that the council "affirms the belief that, in this rich diverse world, each child deserves to grow up in a setting that will increase his/her knowledge and appreciation of varied cultural traditions." The Church Council position identified the factors it felt must be included in a comprehensive plan for Seattle: primarily equity, that the "movement of students and other costs of desegregation should be borne equitably by the White and minority communities"; secondly that the primary mission of the schools is to educate and that "quality education is enhanced by integration"; and finally that sensitivity must be exercised in the area of ethnic heritage. "Every child is entitled to be educated in an accepting environment."[3]

The council felt that Seattle's desegregation plan must be a mandatory one:

While affirming the need for voluntary desegregation and the need for voluntary phases to any plan to reassign students, the unsuccessful history of strictly voluntary desegregation efforts in Seattle convinces us that involuntary strategies may have to be employed and we urge their early development by the district.[4]

The practical application of the council's philosophy of pluralism was outlined by the council. "Schools which are presently identified with minority communities must maintain sufficient numbers of minority students in order that their racial identity can be maintained."[5] This statement was amplified by listing those schools which would be allowed to remain between fifty and sixty percent black, the one school which would remain fifty to sixty percent Asian, and those schools which were segregated and served both an Asian and a black population. These would be lidded with approximately one-third black, one-third Asian, and one-third white students (with no group allowed to exceed forty percent). This position was in contrast to a full integration position which would spread racial minority students throughout the district.

A number of other issues were raised in the Church Council position statement, including an open process of community involvement, emphasis on human relations training for staff, students and parents, emphasis on using the district's Affirmative Action Plan to increase the number of minority staff in the district to equal the percentage of minority students, and continual support for specific programs which meet the needs of minority students, including the American Indian Heritage Program, bilingual programs and compensatory education programs. The statement also raised the issue of segregated housing as a contributory factor in school segregation.

Finally, the council committed itself to help.

The Church Council of Greater Seattle and area churches will serve as instruments for raising the moral issues involved, will conduct vigorous community discussions and will serve as a reconciling force in these challenging times. We intend to be advocates for racial justice in education. The welfare of our children and the future of our city will be strongly influenced by the actions taken regarding school desegregation in the coming year. The issues are difficult; the best course of action will not always be clear; people of deep conviction will differ.... If we apply our best energies we may ultimately be moving to the realization, in Seattle, of a truly pluralistic society.[6]

On December 22, 1976, the Church Council statement was read to the Seattle School Board by a representative group from the council, including Edward Iwamoto, pastor of Blaine Memorial Methodist Church, Cecil Murray, pastor of First AME Church, William Cate, president/director of the Church Council of Greater Seattle, and Ann Siqueland. John Cornelius, pastor of St. Mary's Catholic Church and president of BUCFA, also made a statement at the Board meeting regarding the Church Council's statement. In the audience at the School Board meeting were approximately thirty clergy members, including four denominational heads, complete with clerical collars.

On the morning of the School Board meeting, William Cate became aware that the black community leadership could not unanimously support the Church Council's statement. As he recalls:

I received a call in the morning of the day of the presentation from Father John [Cornelius]. John said that they could not support our concept of having some schools where the minority could be in the majority. They wanted an integrated school policy following the NAACP's. All I could say was, "Well, if that's your position, go ahead." But I talked to Chip [Cecil Murray] and he didn't bring that out; he made the presentation. We gave the impression of a totally solid front, even though there was a little crack in it. And it was Meredith Mathews, Walt Hubbard, and Judge Charles Johnson [Central Area Civil Rights Committee] who had taken the integrationist position. They were loyal to the NAACP position. Our plan was different, with a focus on diversity and pluralism. The black clergy [BUCFA] agreed with our position, but they didn't want to publicly break the black unity. They never publicly stated that position. They pulled it off beautifully, for which I was eternally grateful. I had the feeling that they wouldn't even show up. But they did.... When I got that word early in the morning, that was my most traumatic moment of the Church Council's efforts to help bring about desegregation.[7]

The disagreement over desegregation strategies surfaced as a result of the meeting of the Asian and black leadership organized by Cecil Murray. At the meeting, the general statement that schools could retain a majority of racial minority students was expanded to list individual schools and the racial minority percentage desired in each school. The revision was the result of a suggestion from Murray and was different from the national NAACP position of full integration. With the Church Council's position outlined so specifically, it was not possible for members of the Central Area Rights Committee to support it.

At the School Board presentation it appeared that BUCFA was endorsing the Church Council's statement, when in fact the difference of opinion over strategies to achieve integration had surfaced that day in the black community. Throughout the discussion of a desegregation plan for Seattle, the debate over strategies ranging from "black separation" to full integration continued in the black community, but never surfaced publicly.

Don Daughtry reflected on the Church Council's efforts to model its stated goal of pluralism:

One of the things we did was to share leadership. Our image was one of a pluralistic society; that's what we're working for. So, whenever we approached the administration, the School Board, or anybody, we did it with Asians, blacks and Caucasians. We never sent an all-black group in or an all-white group. We were working for a pluralistic society, so we lived that ourselves.[8]

As Cate recalls:

I believe, as I look back on it, that that was one of the important roles we played, if not *the* most important role at the early stage. We provided a place where Asians and blacks could get together and talk, and where whites could talk with them about desegregation and establish some common goals together. We didn't have our big internal battle in front of the School Board. When they saw us, they saw a common front. There was probably less of a common front than they thought. There was never a situation prior to that where we had worked together with BUCFA. Prior to that we had never done any community program together as a group. It was the first time the Church Council had been such an effective forum.[9]

This dialogue between Asian, black and white members of the community, resulting in the statement on pluralism, provided the initial philosophical basis for the Seattle Plan. As Arlene Oki recalls:

I felt that the Racial Justice in Education Committee, more than any other committee, established certain criteria under which the plan would be adopted. And three of these things were: the definition of racial imbalance, the equity of student movement, and the need for multicultural education; those were all included in the statement that was presented to the School Board. I think it was the first time a group had gone before the Board with some specifics, some kind of detail of what should be included in a mandatory plan.[10]

In fact, the Church Council's statement included ideas from various segments of the community, from individuals and groups which had a long-standing interest in and commitment to desegregation.

The full impact of the statement was felt later as its ideas were incorporated into the criteria developed by DWAC and the School Board[11] for a desegregation plan. The statement also formed the basis for all subsequent activities of the Church Council, providing representatives of the council with a strong and well-defined position to work from throughout the process of developing the Seattle Plan. It also formed the basis for a considerable amount of adult education which began in February 1977 in Seattle area churches and continued through the implementation of the plan in September of 1978.

At the time the Church Council developed its statement on pluralism, at least two possible definitions of a segregated school existed. One was the definition adopted by Washington State, which stated that a school was to be considered segregated when the population of a single minority group reached forty percent. Because of the multiracial nature of the Seattle Public Schools, by this definition a school without a single white student would not be considered segregated if the proportions of other races were, for instance, thirty-nine percent black, thirty-nine percent Asian American, eleven percent Hispanic, and eleven percent Native American. No school in the district existed with this composition, but a number existed which had both a large black population and a large Asian American population. The second definition was included in the federal guidelines for Title VII of the Emergency School Aid Act. By this definition, a school was considered segregated when its combined racial minority population exceeded fifty percent, which would mean that any school which did not house at least fifty percent white students was segregated. Many more schools in Seattle were segregated by this federal definition than by the Washington State definition, necessitating more student transfers to end segregation. In addition the federal definition did not recognize the individual identity of separate racial minority groups. For many minority people this definition denied a sense of individual racial identity.

The Church Council position violated both federal and state definitions, and the task force felt that it must determine if its position statement could survive legal scrutiny. The basic philosophical issue, irrespective of the specific numbers or percentages of students outlined in the Church Council position, was the idea that students should be able to meet one another in a school environment on the basis of numerical parity. Each racial group should be represented in approximately equal numbers. In order for this to happen, it would be necessary to have a dual definition for segregation, one that would apply to schools in the central area, which housed a predominately black population (in the range of ninety percent in some schools) and another which would apply to schools in the southeast area of the city, which housed both a large black and a large Asian American population.

Virginia Balderama from the local Office of Civil Rights (Region X) was invited to a meeting of the task force to discuss the council's position in relation to the definition of racial imbalance or segregation. Because the federal government had required full integration of the teaching staff in Seattle, the task force wanted to know what position it was likely to take concerning student integration. Arlene Oki invited about twenty Asian American community people who had been active in local schools in the southeast area to the meeting. Balderama in essence told the task force and community members that the federal government did not have one specific definition for segregation; a variety of definitions had been used across the country resulting from various court decisions. The Title VII definition was intended for use in awarding desegregation funds. While making it clear that she could not speak for the Office of Civil Rights, Balderama felt that the

Church Council's definition, if used in a citywide desegregation plan, would probably satisfy the Office of Civil Rights. The task force members left the meeting feeling that the Church Council's position was legally defensible.

The definition of racial imbalance later adopted by the Seattle School Board retained the concept of a dual definition. However, the percentage of racial minority students permitted in a school was tied to a percentage of the districtwide minority population on the advice of the school district legal counsel.

When the Church Council urged the Seattle School Board to "proceed with all deliberate speed," on December 22, 1976, to end public school segregation, it also committed itself to help by providing educational programs in Seattle area churches. An extensive adult education program was initiated with the assistance of a grant from the Washington Commission for the Humanities and funds from church denominational sources. During the eighteen months of the program, adult education classes and forums were held in a hundred churches in the greater Seattle area. Three editions of a hundred-page curriculum guide and resource book were printed, and two slide shows were produced. Workshops were held for teachers from individual congregations, speakers were provided to churches, and presentations were made to groups of clergy meeting by denomination. The program was coordinated by Ann Siqueland with the assistance of task force members, numerous volunteers, and for a period by a Mennonite volunteer, Nancy Carlin. The program utilized the expertise of academic humanists in writing the resource book, planning the program, and speaking at churches. The adult education classes were probably the most extensive ecumenical education effort ever conducted in Seattle, reaching probably thirty-five hundred people individually in adult classes, and additional thousands through radio, television and the print media. The program also encouraged local pastors to address the subject of desegregation in sermons, and two tapes were prepared of theological discussions by ecumenical groups of clergy on desegregation and the church's role and responsibility in this area. It is difficult to assess the impact that the Church Council's educational program had on the climate of the city, or the extent to which it helped prepare people for what was to come. David Colwell, the pastor of Plymouth Congregational Church in Seattle, became cochair of the Task Force on Racial Justice in the spring of 1977 when Daughtry accepted a call to the Hawaiian Islands. He reflected on this matter:

Pastors in various places and lay people had the stand of the Church Council before them, which made them rethink where they might be. I don't know, and I don't suppose we can ever find out, how many statements of support, how many sermons and things like that during that period, were preached in various and sundry congregations large and small on this issue, but I'm sure that there were a number. I have the feeling that this was a part of the reason that we got things done as well as we did. There were a lot of church folks who had to face the fact that responsible people in leadership roles had a position on desegregation and though they might not totally agree with it, they had to deal with it instead of just reacting in an automatic way, negatively.[12]

Having gotten out of a melting pot philosophy of public education, the Church Council soon found itself jumping into the fire of court action. Although the initial impetus for the Church Council's activity in desegregation efforts was a reaction to the possibility of court-ordered desegregation through an investigation of student-assignment policies by the Office of Civil Rights, the lack of significant movement toward mandatory forms of desegregation by the Seattle School Board led the council by March of 1977 to consider becoming a plaintiff in a lawsuit filed against the school district.

Most of the discussion about desegregation on the part of the superintendent, administration and School Board during the 1976–77 school year had revolved around the concept of developing magnet schools which would seek to draw voluntary student movement by providing special program incentives. However, there was also discussion during this time of the need for a "contingency plan," some sort of backup to the voluntary magnet approach which would assure that sufficient student transfers occurred to substantially desegregate the schools. When the School Board adopted the Magnet School Plan on March 7, 1977, with no backup contingency plan, a high level of frustration was experienced by many members of the Church Council task force. Seattle had been in the process of voluntarily desegregating its schools since 1963, but the schools were becoming increasingly segregated.

By March 1977, Cecil Murray and David Colwell were cochairing the Church Council task force. During one task force meeting in March, the subject of what to do in the light of the Magnet Plan was discussed. If the School Board did not act to end segregation in Seattle, it seemed likely that, either through action of the federal government, or as a result of a suit filed by the NAACP and the ACLU, Seattle would be desegregated by court order. The nature of a court-ordered plan, which might not take into consideration the uniqueness of Seattle, especially its multiracial (rather than biracial) population, was a continual concern of the task force, along with their concern that a court-ordered plan might result in a citywide dispersion of minority students like that of the teacher transfers. The ACLU did not have a stated philosophy or approach to desegregation, but was looking instead for "significant movement." The NAACP, however, did have a national position of full integration which differed from the Church Council's position. Task force members felt that if the decision on a desegregation plan was to be settled in the courts, as members of the plaintiff group, the Church Council would be in a position to negotiate for its position, either through a compromise plan developed before a court ruling or as part of any plan a judge might develop. The Church Council had never been involved in litigation before, and contemplating this action was considered a serious matter by task force members.

The conversation regarding the possibility of becoming involved in litigation continued into a second task force meeting. In the meantime Cecil Murray, Bill Cate and Ann Siqueland met with Lacy Steele of the NAACP to discuss the NAACP's position on desegregation. They were assured that, despite some differences of opinion within the Seattle chapter, should the NAACP become involved in a suit against the Seattle School Board, the organization would argue in court for the national NAACP position of full integration; however, the Church Council could join in a suit. Conversations with the ACLU were also begun and the idea of the council's participating in a possible suit was received very favorably. David Harrison, executive director of the ACLU of Washington, agreed to attend the next task force meeting, outline the process for litigation and discuss a possible agreement between joint plaintiffs.

At the next meeting of the task force, following the presentation of information by David Harrison, Cecil Murray asked each member to express his or her own opinion regarding the possibility of becoming involved in a lawsuit. With one exception, the members of the task force, including Bill Cate, felt that joining the suit was the best course of action available, and that the action would be consistent with accomplishing the goals of the Church Council. The task force decided to recommend to the board of directors of the Church Council that the council become a plaintiff in a lawsuit charging the Seattle Public Schools with illegal segregation. Furthermore, in the spirit of its method for developing the statement on pluralism, task force members decided to discuss the possibility of a joint suit with other community groups.

Most of the community groups represented on DWAC were invited to a meeting at the Church Council offices in early April. Of those invited, representatives of the Seattle Urban League, JACL, the League of Women Voters, the American Friends Service Committee, AAEA, and a group of Asian lawyers attended the meeting to hear a presentation by attorney Fred Noland and David Harrison from the ACLU on the legal issues involved in a suit, the funds required, and the particulars of a joint agreement between the plaintiffs. A process was developed for joint decision-making among the organizations and for informing the community of the expanded interest in the lawsuit. A press release was prepared listing the interested organizations and the dates of the upcoming board meetings of each, at which a vote would be taken to authorize litigation. When the press release was issued, only the names of the NAACP, the ACLU, the Church Council (including BUCFA) and AAEA appeared. While not listed, the Urban League had also clearly indicated that, if a suit was ever filed, it would be a party. Each of the groups listed in the press release, including the Church Council, did authorize participation in a suit.

The increased activity aimed at bringing about desegregation through a lawsuit triggered a considerable amount of activity on the part of groups such as the Municipal League and the Chamber of Commerce (see Chapter 9). Other community groups had already been actively supporting desegregation in various ways.

CHAPTER 6

SUPPORT FROM MANY GROUPS

Support for desegregation was developing in community groups which did not participate in the threat of litigation. Among these were Seattle Council PTSA, the League of Women Voters, the American Friends Service Committee and the People Power Coalition.

Seattle Council PTSA

The Seattle Council PTSA (Parent-Teacher-Student Association), of the organizations which participated in discussions which led up to the adoption of the Seattle Plan, is probably the most geographically and ideologically representative of the general population in Seattle. Its membership includes the parents of children attending Seattle Public Schools and Seattle teachers. Concerning its representativeness, it should also be said that PTSA does not include a proportionate number of black, Asian, or other racial minority group individuals. Some schools in the inner city rely on what are termed parent groups instead of PTSAs.

During the time that middle school desegregation was taking place in Seattle, Seattle Council PTSA, which includes representatives from individual school building PTSAs, plus a board, became involved in the controversy over that mandatory approach to desegregation. Ellen Roe, later to become a member of the School Board, and several individuals actively opposed to middle school desegregation were on the board of Seattle Council PTSA at the time, and as a result PTSA Council took a position of opposing mandatory busing in 1970–71.

Kay Groves, who served as president of Seattle Council PTSA from 1976 to 1978, recalls that period:

When Citizens Against Mandatory Busing was active, PTSA Council took a position in support of the CAMB position. They would support voluntary desegregation, not mandatory. That attitude stayed with the council probably until 1975 or so.

I became president after being first vice-president and before that, human relations chairperson.

Before I had come to Seattle Council I had been on the Ingraham Area Advisory Committee[1] [in far northwest Seattle where Groves lives]. There I began to realize that I didn't agree with people who opposed mandatory desegregation, though I was not a very strong voice.

While Barbara Beuschlein[2] became president [in 1974–76] there was about a 180-degree turn on council with maybe sixty percent of the executive committee realizing that voluntary desegregation wasn't working. The district couldn't afford to go through voluntary recruitment every year.

Ellen Roe was the secretary of council the first year Barbara was president. She resigned when she was elected to the School Board, and probably when Ellen left, most of the CAMB people left too.[3]

The same day that the Church Council of Greater Seattle's board of directors adopted a statement of pluralism which encouraged, among other things, the use of mandatory means to desegregate schools, a similar motion was passed by the PTSA Council. Groves recalls:

It was on December 14, 1976. The motion was presented by Don Daughtry.[4] He and his wife were the delegates to council from their school. He presented the motion, and it was passed with very little debate and very little altering of the original motion. We had a lot of people there, and the motion had not been presented ahead of time. Normally if anything comes up that makes people a little bit uncomfortable, it is referred to committee and reported back the next month. But it passed! That was a real shock.

That was a year before the Seattle Plan was adopted, and the motion was that voluntary strategies would be supported first, realizing that a mandatory backup would be necessary. There were fourteen points to the motion. The only one the Seattle Plan doesn't address is the use of voluntary means first.[5]

Actually the motion passed because Groves, chairing the meeting in Barbara Beuschlein's absence, cast the tie-breaking vote. However, the council did not hold the vote against Groves because she was elected council president for two years the following spring.

The council was represented on DWAC by Barbara Beuschlein, Kay

Groves, Judith Youngman (PTSA president at McDonald Elementary School in the near north central part of Seattle), and Susan Wallace (PTSA president at Wedgwood Elementary School in the northeastern part of Seattle). The elementary schools in the neighborhoods where all four PTSA members resided were to become paired or triaded schools under the Seattle Plan,[6] as did many other schools attended by children of DWAC members. Though no one can remember that this happened by design, it does indicate that DWAC was not involved in desegregation planning for "other people." It also meant that members of DWAC were often closely involved in the local communities which experienced desegregation firsthand.

The League of Women Voters

The League of Women Voters of Seattle has a long history of interest in public school education in Seattle and public school desegregation efforts. The national league has a long-standing commitment to racial integration in schools as a necessary condition for equal access to quality education, and leagues all over the country have been active in desegregation planning. The league's national position is as follows:

Members of the League of Women Voters of the United States believe the federal government shares with other levels of government responsibility to provide equality of opportunity for education, employment and housing for all persons in the United States. Employment opportunities in modern, technological societies are closely related to education; therefore, the League supports federal programs to increase the education and training of disadvantaged people. The League also supports federal efforts to prevent and/or remove discrimination in education and employment and housing and to help communities bring about racial integration of their school systems.[7]

The Seattle league appointed Peg Williams as a representative on DWAC when that advisory body was appointed in late 1974. Williams served as the chair of the league's Education Action Task Force.

By December 8, 1976, the league was urging the School Board to use mandatory strategies to desegregate schools. In a letter of that date delivered to the School Board, the league said:

The School Board has taken a strong position that desegregation will be accomplished and we are delighted. We believe, however, that the concept of a mandatory back-up to a voluntary strategy is necessary. Seattle's past experience as well as the experience in other parts of the country, indicate that there may need to be mandatory aspects if voluntary strategies do not produce the desired results and we urge the Board to give the Desegregation Planning Task Force[8] the go ahead for back-up mandatory planning.[9]

The following month, in January 1977, when DWAC lost its chair, Dan Levant, Peg Williams assumed the responsibility of securing a new chairperson for the group since no one else on the committee wanted to take the responsibility. Williams approached Jerome Page, executive director of the Seattle Urban League, for suggestions. Page asked Richard Andrews, the chair of the Urban League's Education Committee, if he would be willing to assume the responsibility. Andrews agreed after meeting with DWAC.

When the School Board adopted the voluntary Magnet School Plan in March of 1977, the league supported the plan. According to Austrid Hedman, who became league president in June of 1977:

We committed some Rowntree Money,[10] a very precious pot of money, for the production of a pamphlet on the plan so that people could become aware of the magnet program and its impact. Our hopes were very high.[11]

The league's pamphlet received wide circulation and was an effective tool for gathering community support for desegregation and the Magnet Plan. The pamphlet was a four-page brochure on the plan.

However, by May it was apparent that the Magnet Plan was not going to solve Seattle's problem of segregated schools, and the league addressed the School Board on May 25:

We reiterate our support for the efforts of the district to find a solution to the problem of increasing segregation of Seattle schools. The magnet plan, even though the immediate goal of 1,000 new transfers is achieved, cannot by itself desegregate schools such as Leschi, nor will the magnet plan acccomplish its goal in schools where, for one reason or another, recruitment is lagging.[12]

In April the league had been invited by the Church Council of Greater Seattle to discuss the possibility of participating in legal action against the School Board to bring about the end to segregation. While attending a meeting to discuss the subject and conducting some research into the league's position on litigation across the country, Astrid Hedman, when she became league president in June 1977, did not feel that she or members of the new board of the league were informed on the issue well enough to participate in a lawsuit.

American Friends Service Committee

When communities discussed the possibility of desegregating their schools, the subject of involving students in the decisions which were being made was often raised at one point or another.

The American Friends Service Committee (AFSC) in Seattle did work with a multiracial group of high school students from a geographic cross-section of the city to involve them in the discussions about desegregation. The project was called SAFE, Student Action Force on Education.

The impetus for AFSC's participation in desegregation efforts came both from discussions with others in Seattle, and from a national AFSC conference. Jonis Davis served as the education staff person with AFSC beginning in 1976. She recalls the Service Committee's process for defining desegregation as a priority issue and the initiation of the SAFE project.

In 1976 the national AFSC announced that they were having a "roundup" of people working in education and would like someone from each region to go. I went to that meeting representing the Northwest. The meeting was held in Georgia in March, and almost everyone who came was working on desegregation-related projects.

One of the results of the week-long meeting was a recommendation to the national board of AFSC that it reaffirm its commitment to desegregation as a means through which all people would be able to succeed in American society. At the end of April, 1976, they did pass a fairly lengthy "minute," the AFSC term for resolution, restating this commitment.

I came back from the meeting really electrified. One of the funny things that I learned was that people were unaware that Seattle had desegregated its middle schools with a mandatory program without a court order. I had not realized how extremely rare we were in the country.

In part, as a result of my report, the Northwest region of AFSC decided that it should be addressing the area of education and directed me to put together a task force to consider what useful role we might play.

In June we assembled about twelve people for the task force with Sarah Welch as chair, including students, teachers and parents. It met every two weeks, and the meetings were long. We researched and talked at some length about issues such as bilingual education, basic skills, discipline, student rights, minimum competency and desegregation.

We invited Dan Levant, then chair of DWAC, to one meeting, and he was very helpful in providing information on desegregation. I occasionally went to a DWAC meeting.

After Dick Andrews became the chair of DWAC, it became very clear that desegregation was going to be happening, and we decided in about March of 1977 to make desegregation our primary concern.

During that year we had been meeting with students from Garfield, Lincoln, and Franklin high schools to get a sense from them of the issues they were facing. We got some very candid comments on desegregation. One of the things that became clear was that, although students are the ones who experience desegregation, they were not involved in making decisions. That's when we decided to focus on high school students and created the SAFE project.[13]

In the summer of 1977, AFSC recruited students and paid them with funds from the Summer Youth Employment Program and funds from the AFSC national Youth Involvement Fund. Originally the program was to develop a telephone hot line on which students could call other students to ask questions and give opinions about desegregation. The focus of the program eventually developed along different lines as the result of the expressed desires of the students. According to Davis:

The summer program was going to run eight or ten weeks, and we knew that we had to start with training the students. We had quite a detailed structured plan that involved a certain amount of reading and bringing people in to talk with the group, attending School Board meetings and interviewing school district administrators.

We also had a lot of group process activities because we knew that it wasn't going to be easy to have such a diverse group of students working together. Actually this continued as a knotty, unresolvable problem. Sometimes it worked, and sometimes it didn't work. Things never entirely broke down, but it was something we had to work through all the time.

After three or so days on this strict schedule, the kids said they wanted to meet by themselves without the staff. We said, "Fine." When we came back, they had organized the project, saying they wanted to focus on six or seven issues. (They happened to be the same issues the task force had focused on the previous year.) We were thrilled, and they took off.

They worked in high gear for a couple of weeks. Some of the groups were able to follow through and some were not, or they would hit a snag and not know how to proceed.

But there were several things that happened that summer. They did produce a regular newsletter. And they decided that one member would run for the School Board. They elected Chris Beeson to do that, and he went and talked to his parents and they agreed. The students called a press conference and explained why they felt a student should be on the School Board. They all went together down to the courthouse to attempt to file, and although Chris was turned down because he was too young, it was a very dynamic project.

They also tried to arrange for student representation on DWAC, but didn't follow through.[14]

One of the issues the SAFE group became interested in was student suspension; some of the SAFE students had been suspended from school — unfairly, they thought — and they decided that they wanted to find out about the district's suspension policies and data on who and how many were suspended. Initially they had some difficulty, as Davis recalls:

The district said that they couldn't share the information with the students. So a couple of them went down to the office of the ACLU and got a copy of the public disclosure act and quoted it in a letter to the district. They were successful in getting the documents, and that was a major victory.[15]

Although the SAFE project was originally intended as a summer program, the students remained together during most of the 1977–78 school year and the summer of 1978.

AFSC also considered joining with other community groups in a suit to bring about desegregation in the spring of 1977. Their decision not to participate came as a result of a discussion with members of the black community, with which AFSC had actively worked. According to Davis:

When we knew that a lawsuit was being considered, naturally we raised the question of whether or not we should join. Members of our task force were quite ambivalent about desegregation. We were aware of the struggles of black people who were in desegregated settings and were being bused. We were also conscious of the fact that the momentum for the lawsuit was coming from "white liberals," particularly the ACLU. It was not clear who NAACP was representing. They didn't seem to represent the blacks we were talking to.

Because the basic assumption is that desegregation is to help the black community, we wanted to reflect the attitudes of the people we were working with. There was enough hesitation and enough uncertainty that we decided it was not appropriate for us to participate in the lawsuit.[16]

People Power Coalition

Emory Bundy, public affairs director of KING-TV in Seattle, and William Cate, president/director of the Church Council of Greater Seattle, organized the People Power Coalition in 1971 as an avenue for the media to participate in discussions of current community issues. The board of the coalition is composed of representatives of about thirty community organizations including the Municipal League, the League of Women Voters, the Church Council, the Seattle Urban League, PTSA, the ACLU, the Anti-Defamation League, city and county government, community councils, etc., as well as representatives from various segments of the media, specifically KING, Channel 9 (public television in Seattle), and KZAM Radio.

In April of 1975, Arlis Stewart became the director of the coalition. Stewart was hired to direct a project entitled "The New Birth of Freedom," an attempt to stimulate discussions of American democracy during the bicentennial. With a grant from the Washington Commission for the Humanities, using the services of academic humanists, the coalition sponsored a number of forums that dealt with local issues within the context of the basic values and political perceptions upon which the United States was founded.

In the fall of 1976 when the coalition began to discuss what issue it would next address, public school desegregation surfaced as the most pressing issue which would be facing Seattle. The reassignment and desegregation of Seattle's teaching corps, brought about by pressure from the federal government in 1976, with the indication from HEW that Seattle's student-assignment policies would soon be under investigation, as well as the fact that the district had hired a new superintendent, David Moberly, seemed to indicate that desegregation would soon be addressed again in Seattle.

By December the coalition had decided to seek funding to conduct community forums on the issue of desegregation, and in January an application of intent to submit a proposal was submitted to the Washington Commission for the Humanities. Simultaneously the Church Council of Greater Seattle had determined that it would be seeking funding to conduct an adult-education program in Seattle area churches on desegregation. The two programs were combined in the request for funding from the commission. People Power would coordinate informational programming through the print and electronic media and conduct general community forums, and the Church Council would develop a series of forums and adult classes to be held in local churches.

In preparation for the People Power program, Arlis Stewart called a series of meetings to which representatives from various community organizations who had an interest in desegregation were invited. The group was to identify desegregation-related issues which would be discussed in the proposed People Power forums. These meetings helped define the scope of the People Power program and also developed into an ongoing series of meetings between various community organization representatives which continued on a regular basis from January to June, 1977. These discussions, along with others taking place on the DWAC, served as a communication link between groups who were interested in bringing about an end to segregation. The People Power meetings were attended by individuals representing organizations not represented at that time on DWAC — specifically the ACLU, the City of Seattle, the Municipal League, and the Chamber of Commerce. Several of the People Power meetings discussed the pros and cons of court-ordered desegregation. Since members of the press were always present at the discussions, the meetings served as a means of creating public awareness. Arlis Stewart recalls:

We decided we needed a mechanism whereby the key players in organizations involved in desegregation could meet on a regular basis, discuss the issues as they were developing, level with each other about what they were doing, record those discussions and distribute them widely so that the media would start to get a broader base of information on the subject. We also wanted antagonists to face the public together. At that time [in early 1977] David Moberly would say, "xyz" with regard to the possibility of a lawsuit, and David Harrison of ACLU would say "pdq" about what someone had reported that David Moberly had said. But you never had those two together in the same room with the media there. We wanted to do that sort of thing.[17]

Stewart also joined DWAC and a number of other groups. As she says:

One of the things that happens when People Power has totally jumped into an issue, is that Arlis has managed to get herself appointed to almost every relevant advisory committee because that's one of the ways you keep track of things.[18]

Stewart jumped into things.

Stewart also had served on the steering committee which had conducted Cheryl Bleakney's campaign for the School Board in 1975, and she lived in the Queen Anne Hill area Bleakney represented. She spent a considerable amount of time discussing desegregation with Bleakney, keeping her intimately informed about what was taking place in community discussions on desegregation. Bleakney was able to take a leadership role on the School Board, partly because she was kept so well informed on what was happening in the community. In turn, through discussions with Bleakney, Stewart kept some individuals, especially members of DWAC, informally informed about where the School Board was heading.

In addition, Stewart spend a considerable amount of time at the school district offices, as she says,

> making a general pest of myself. We would go down to the school district, and when they said, "We don't have the information" I wanted, I'd say, "Yes, you do; it's over here." It got to the point that by April whenever we asked for information, it came fairly easily because that was easier for them than having us ask for it again and again.[19]

Among other things, People Power conducted six forums in downtown Seattle during March, April and May of 1977 at the Metro YMCA on the subject of desegregation litigation. As Stewart recalls:

> We brought William Taylor[20] here on April 17, 18, and 19 for two reasons. Number one, he was a person who had been involved in promoting litigation to solve the problem of racial imbalance in school districts across the country. He was knowledgeable and had participated in litigation. He thoroughly believed that litigation was not the worst thing that could happen because it was a way to get the job done.
>
> Secondly, he was a person who was knowledgeable about the relationship between housing segregation and school desegregation.
>
> Taylor felt that school districts under court order to desegregate did not lose much control unless they were absolutely hostile to the court. He could describe a number of districts where things had gone rather well as a result of litigation. Litigation brought people together who really had a lot of things in common, but had previously only dwelt on their differences.
>
> We had a very good turnout for the brown bag discussions with William Taylor. Taylor was shaking his head by the time he left Seattle, saying, "Well, maybe you folks are the ones who can do it yourselves without litigation. It will be nice, but I'll believe it when I see it."[21]

Shan Mullin and Eben Carlson (see Chapter 9) and others from the Municipal League had participated in the discussions with Taylor. Mullin was convinced, contrary to Taylor's belief, that Seattle could desegregate its schools without a court order and that it would be better for Seattle to take action on its own.

The People Power forums discussed the possibility of court-ordered desegregation at the time groups who were preparing to sue the district were beginning to take serious steps which would lead to court action. The NAACP had filed a complaint with the Office of Civil Rights, charging that the district was illegally segregated, on April 20. Other organizations were considering joining the NAACP and the ACLU in the suit. The People Power forums brought the Municipal League face-to-face with possible plaintiffs for the first time. The media covered the forums well, and the forums were one of the factors which focused the issues surrounding litigation and helped several individuals to make the decision that they would encourage the School Board to take the necessary steps to eliminate segregation by its own action, rather than allow a court to decide the issue.

Beginning in January 1977, Stewart also began to work with the elementary school parents in the area where she lived to develop support for desegregation. Hay Elementary School on Queen Anne Hill had recognized that desegregation would become an issue in Seattle as the result of the HEW staff transfers carried out in 1976. A black principal, Orie Green, was assigned to Hay. Hay parents had begun to develop a volunteer school pairing with Brighton Elementary School in southeast Seattle in 1977, having concluded that the school district's Magnet Plan would weaken their school. Stewart had lived in the area all of her life. By discussing desegregation intensely, the Hay community eventually developed a position on desegregation which paralleled the position taken by DWAC, demonstrating that the possibility exists for community members, once they develop some experience with desegregation, to realize that mandatory plans are the most desirable and effective approach. As Stewart recalls:

The community in my neighborhood began the discussion about desegregation from a strictly "voluntary only" point of view. We spent a lot of time and effort wrestling internally with the issue and coming to terms with the facts.

This is a fact which amazed me about a number of people and organizations. Where people were willing for a period of time to set aside their original biases and look at the history and the facts of the situation, many came to realize the limitations of a voluntary plan such as the Magnet Plan. People could see that you needed a structural systemwide approach, rather than a patchwork approach to desegregate schools.

Hay developed a voluntary pairing and recruited about thirty-five students to transfer schools. But it took an awful lot of work, and people realized that a mandatory transfer would be better and easier, as long as neighborhood children of the same age continued to go to school together.

The potential support for desegregation existed in that one little neighborhood with a severely declining enrollment. If you had asked me a week before I got involved if I felt it was likely that I would find many folks who were interested in discussing desegregation and supporting it, I would have said, "Not a chance." But I was wrong. There were all kinds of closet civil rights people in my neighborhood.[22]

A similar discovery had been made by individuals supportive of desegregation during the time the Middle School Plan was being developed. The debate over the citywide Seattle Plan took place in numerous communities across the city during 1977, and although these discussions were often more heated than the one in the Hay community, individuals who were willing to support the desegregation of schools were able to organize support for the plan in virtually all communities.

CHAPTER 7

THE LEGAL THREAT: PRESSURE TO DECIDE

Extensive support for desegregation did exist in Seattle, but it took the threat of the heavy hand of the law to bring about action. Along with the NAACP, the ACLU attempted early to influence the School Board with the most effective method available, a lawsuit. It worked.

It also must be said that a lawsuit was not necessarily viewed as the most desirable way to desegregate Seattle Public Schools by the groups threatening to sue. Dan Levant, who worked with the ACLU on their potential lawsuit, after resigning as the chair of the DWAC, always said that the best way to avoid a lawsuit was to unconditionally plan to file one.[1] And much of ACLU's activity during 1976 and 1977 was not only taking all the necessary steps to prepare for a suit, but letting as many people as possible know exactly what ACLU was planning. This strategy worked. The suit never had to be filed. A look at ACLU activity during 1976 indicates the preparation which preceded ACLU's legal threat.

Discussions about desegregation were intensified within the ACLU of Washington during 1976. Attorney Fred Noland believes that renewed interest in desegregation within the local ACLU was the result of discussions on that subject at the national level.[2] The national ACLU has a long-established policy on public school segregation and has participated in litigation against numerous school districts aimed at ending segregation. In a memo from the Washington ACLU's Committee on Seattle School Desegregation, July 5, 1976, to the state ACLU's board of directors, the committee decided to accept the existing national ACLU policy which strongly supported the governing principle of *Brown* v. *Board of Education* that "separate educational facilities are inherently unequal," and viewed the following as appropriate methods to end segregation:

1. Zoning of cities for integration;
2. Selection of new school sites to further integration;
3. Reclassification of schools, as to grade levels;
4. Busing as an appropriate affirmative action to overcome segregation; and
5. Alteration or disregard of school district boundaries where integration within particular school districts is impossible.

During the summer of 1976, prior to the July memo to the ACLU board, the Committee on Seattle School Desegregation, chaired by Jim Tyler, had been discussing the issue of staff integration of the Seattle School District required by HEW.

In the summer of 1975 the Department of Health, Education and Welfare had found that the district had not complied with the assurances in the guidelines under which the district received desegregation funds (Title VII, Emergency School Aid Act), or with the Civil Rights Act, specifically in the areas of assignment of minority teachers and services provided to non-English-speaking students. The district challenged the HEW interpretation of the law and filed suit to obtain federal funds which HEW had withheld as a result of the finding of noncompliance. The school district lost.

Not only did the Seattle School District lose some federal funds during 1975–76, but the loss of the levy in 1975 severely limited the district's financial resources during 1976.

In May of 1976 the ACLU requested information from the school district on the issues of staff segregation and bilingual education. In June, Dr. Harold Reasby, acting superintendent (Loren Troxel had finished his tenure as superintendent, and David Moberly did not arrive in Seattle until August 1976), responded to the ACLU's request with a summary of the events which had taken place. The ACLU then asked for all correspondence relating to the civil rights violation charge from the HEW in June, citing the Freedom of Information Act. Three volumes of information were provided in July. The ACLU also obtained copies of the School Board's new desegregation goals adopted May 19, 1976, which included the statement:

It is the goal of the Seattle School District to accomplish the integration of all schools and programs through a concentrated effort on voluntary strategies, so long as such strategies prove effective, with the Board invoking mandatory strategies to obtain these ends only when voluntary approaches fail to establish integration within an acceptable time frame.[3]

When DWAC was established in late 1975, the ACLU appointed Melinda Selden as its representative to that advisory group. Through DWAC, the ACLU was informed about the activity of other groups interested in desegregation as well as the school district's posture on the issue.

Acting on the request of the ACLU Committee on Seattle School Desegregation, the board of the ACLU adopted the following motion on July 5, 1976:

It is clear that the Seattle School Board has failed to meet its constitutionally-imposed mandate to integrate fully the Seattle school system. The continued existence of racially-identifiable schools is intolerable.[4]

Following the adoption of this resolution, the ACLU reorganized its desegregation committee to include seven practicing attorneys. The new group, called the ACLU Desegregation Task Force, began to meet regularly and discuss the possibility of bringing about the end to segregation through court action. The Desegregation Task Force membership included attorneys Phil Ginsberg, Fred Noland, Phil Burton (also an NAACP attorney), Cynthia Gillespie, Bertha Houser, Charles Corker, and Jim Martell, and nonattorneys Dan Levant and Jim Tyler.

Fred Noland had been out of the country on a sabbatical from March through September 1976. Upon his return home, he became the chair of the ACLU's standing Legal Committee. As a practice, the ACLU uses the volunteer assistance of attorneys to assist with civil liberties legal cases. The Legal Committee meets twice monthly to review requests for assistance and regularly reviews up to six possible cases at each meeting. Because of the extensive involvement of the ACLU in litigation, and because desegregation efforts are most frequently brought about through court action, it was logical that the ACLU would look at the possibility of pursuing desegregation through the courts.

Fred Noland was interested in participating on the reorganized ACLU Desegregation Task Force because he was opposed to the ACLU's becoming involved in desegregation litigation. He wanted to make certain that the ACLU did not jump into a desegregation court battle in a "knee-jerk" manner because of the time-consuming and expensive nature of such litigation, which would require a superhuman effort on the part of ACLU volunteer attorneys. As Noland put it, the $40,000 to $60,000 price tag (for out-of-pocket expenses only, not including lawyers' fees) that could be attached to such litigation was the "Legal Committee's budget for the century."[5]

In an attempt to reason with the school district, ACLU members began a series of meetings with the district in November 1976. About eight members of the ACLU, most of whom were lawyers, first met with Superintendent Moberly and legal counsel Gary Little on November 4, 1976. According to Noland, Moberly took the outrageous position that he did not care if the ACLU sued because the district would win in court, intimating that the district knew where the power was in Washington, D.C., which would keep Seattle off the hook. The voluntary student transfer Magnet Plan, according to Moberly, was an adequate desegregation plan.[6]

Fred Noland left the meeting with Moberly convinced that a lawsuit was a good idea because of the superintendent's attitude. Had Moberly indicated that the district was committed to desegregation, the ACLU would probably have stalled. The ACLU was convinced that any reasonable person could easily understand that voluntary desegregation efforts would never be successful.[7]

During the summer of 1976, David Harrison became the executive director of the American Civil Liberties Union of Washington. He took an active interest in the issue of public school desegregation in Seattle.

In discussing the role that ACLU played in efforts to end segregation in Seattle, Harrison says:

In the beginning we felt we could play a special role by pursuing the litigation threat. The threat of litigation has played a major role in attempts to desegregate all major cities in the country. Seattle wasn't likely to be any different. Through most of the twenty years of failure to desegregate the Seattle schools, there hadn't been a real litigative threat. It was the missing element in 1976 and 1977, and it was a role we could play skillfully. I think we focused on litigation, not so much because we were thrilled about the prospect of taking the City of Seattle to court, but because we felt that that was a unique role that ACLU could play.

For a time, the primary litigative threat was from HEW. It was subject to the weaknesses of a bureaucracy and to some considerable political influence. I don't think we could have left the threat of litigation to HEW and gotten any real results. So we felt that ACLU, working with others such as the NAACP and the Church Council, could provide a strategic element that had not been present in recent years and could help shift the whole issue. And I think we proved to be right.

ACLU was one of literally dozens of organizations in Seattle at that time who had an impact on desegregation. But I believe that ACLU's impact was significant because of the litigative threat. I don't think anyone could maintain that without that threat the Board would have adopted a mandatory desegregation plan.[8]

The strategy of bringing about desegregation through threatened court action, or through an actual suit, was pursued actively by the ACLU from November 1976 on. The strategy included both preparation for a lawsuit, and an extensive communication effort which kept everyone possible informed about the ACLU's possible action.

David Harrison, Fred Noland and other members of the ACLU met regularly with community organizations, the school district, and city government, and participated as well in community forums on desegregation. The Chamber of Commerce, Municipal League, and City of Seattle all reported meetings with members of the ACLU. One series of meetings with community groups took place in November, December and January, and another series in April and May.

On January 18, ACLU members met with Shelly Yapp and staff members from the city's Office of Policy Planning. Fred Noland remembers that the city's attitude at that time was generally supportive of the idea that something ought to be done to desegregate schools, and that the job would best be done by the local body politic making a decision, rather than having desegregation forced down the city's throat by a court order. By this time the city was satisfied that desegregation would not produce significant white or middle-class flight — the major concern the mayor had had about desegregation.[9]

On January 28, 1977, the ACLU again met with the school district's legal counsel. The ACLU was attempting to determine how hard the district would fight if they were sued. The ACLU, according to Fred Noland, left the meeting feeling that Gary Little (school district legal counsel) knew that the district would have problems proving that there was no illegal segregation, that the School Board would make the decision about how hard they would fight in court, and that the district's legal counsel would "recommend reason."[10]

If a lawsuit was filed, the length of time the case would take to try would depend upon the extent to which the School Board fought it. If the Board took the position that it was innocent of any illegal segregation, and did not make the district's files readily available in the case, the court battle would be a lengthy and expensive one. If, however, the district was cooperative, releasing records and even possibly beginning to develop a more aggressive desegregation plan after the case was filed, a negotiated solution to the problem of segregation could be brought about without a lengthy court battle.

Patt Sutton recalls that prior to the adoption of the Middle School

Desegregation Plan, members of the School Board were almost eager to have someone sue them to get desegregation over with, but in 1977 the School Board was not indicating that it wished to be sued. The suit had the potential for dividing the Board as well as the community because some members of the Board, particularly Suzanne Hittman, would not have fought the suit and might have testified against the district.

In order to raise sufficient funds to fight a court battle, it was necessary for plaintiffs to have the support of a cross-section of the city, to be viewed as responsible, and to have genuinely exhausted every other avenue for bringing about desegregation before actually suing. With this end in mind, the ACLU spoke frequently with anyone who would listen, stating that the ACLU wanted to see "significant movement" on the part of the district to end segregation in order to avoid the lawsuit.

David Harrison recalls efforts in 1977 to communicate these issues:

I felt, and I still feel, that it is simply criminal for white children and black children alike to be raised without the opportunity to develop the life skills to deal with each other in some reasonable fashion.

It's not that the school district was just a little bit lazy, or had a sloppy bureaucracy, or just not focused in the way it should have been. It's that the city, through some deliberate actions, and in the absence of some other actions that it should have taken, had allowed segregation to take place; allowed the city to get more and more segregated without doing anything about it. These broken promises were no longer tolerable.

It's hard to sort out the hundreds of media requests we got. Rarely did more than a day go by without receiving a request from the media to answer questions. The media looked at the issue very intelligently. The *P.-I.* and *Times* competition for information was very useful. Gus Angelos and Eric Nalder[11] were trying to squeeze information from us about what we were going to do next.

Every conceivable item that was happening in the city on desegregation was open for discussion. It was an excellent forum for us. We talked at the People Power meetings and some of the other forums prior to the establishment of the No-Name Committee [see Chapter 11]. These were the vehicles for us to make certain that other people understood how serious we were about the litigative threat. At the same time we wanted to let people know that we were not a bunch of crazies; that we were people who felt that segregation had gone on too long, and intended to play a role in doing something about it. It was useful for others to know what we were doing, and at the same time, we were able to learn what other organizations were doing.[12]

From November to May it began to appear more and more likely that a lawsuit would be filed. The school district was intent on carrying through on its voluntary Magnet Plan, not considered by the ACLU to be "significant movement" toward desegregation.

It became clear that preparations should begin for the suit. The ACLU hired a second-year law student, Annette Klapstein, to begin gathering and cataloguing evidence. In an August 1977 memo, Klapstein summarized for David Harrison, Fred Noland, Dan Levant and Ann Siqueland (the Church Council had by June declared its willingness to join in a suit if one was filed) the information she had collected. One paragraph from the memo reads:

We do have a few fairly clear-cut examples of intentional segregation: the Harrison/McGilvra boundary, the High Point boundaries, the building of additions and the massive use of portables in central area schools during the '60's, when both overcrowding and racial imbalance might have been alleviated by the alternative of sending some of these kids to northend schools.[13]

The school district had been cooperative, and the ACLU had not found it difficult to secure information, an indication that Seattle probably would not have fought hard in court if a suit had been filed.

The NAACP and the ACLU were both threatening to sue the school district, and the primary liaison between the two organizations was attorney Phillip Burton, a member of both groups who had worked on desegregation litigation against the school district in the 1960s. David Harrison describes Burton as "a sort of glue that kept the two organizations together." By March 1977, the NAACP and the ACLU were meeting together to discuss the particulars of their cooperative litigation effort. At an April 11 board meeting of the NAACP, formal agreement on joint legal action was taken. The NAACP also decided at that board meeting to file an official civil rights complaint with the Office of Civil Rights, charging that Seattle Public Schools were illegally segregated. Phil Burton wrote the complaint.

By April, other organizations realized that it appeared that desegregation was only going to come about by a court order. The School Board had adopted a voluntary-only desegregation plan unanimously in March, with no "contingency plan" — no backup to complete the job of desegregation if the voluntary effort failed. Feeling that desegregation was going to be decided in the court, the Church Council of Greater Seattle decided to participate in the suit, and began to organize other community groups to participate as well. On April 20, the possibility of an expanded group of joint plaintiffs was discussed by representatives of the Church Council, the JACL, the League of Women Voters, the AFSC, the Seattle Urban League, the AAEA, and a group of Asian lawyers. Fred Noland and David Harrison explained to individuals present the possible scenario of a lawsuit and the details of a cooperative agreement which would be worked out between plaintiffs. Fred Noland would be the lead attorney in the case. Organizational representatives went back to their respective organizations to gain approval for a joint press release and approval to litigate.

On May 4 a meeting was held between lawyers and the leadership of the NAACP to further discuss the joint lawsuit. Members of the NAACP present included Lacy Steele, Seattle branch president; Connie Herring, NAACP representative on DWAC; Judge Charles Johnson; Don Haley, an attorney; Don Smith, assistant athletic director at the University of Washington; and Phil Burton, NAACP attorney. From the ACLU, Dan Levant; David Harrison, executive director; and attorneys Cynthia Gillespie, Phil Ginsberg, and Fred Noland. A second meeting of the same group took place on May 9. The processes for filing a lawsuit were well in motion.

The month of May was a turning point. Up to that time, momentum to bring about desegregation through a lawsuit had progressively grown as a result of inactivity on the part of the School Board. By May, in response to the threatened lawsuit, other forces were mobilized which influenced the School Board to take action to avoid a lawsuit, and thereby desegregate schools by its own action. The mayor of Seattle led the way.

CHAPTER 8

WITHOUT SUPPORT OF CITY GOVERNMENT...

Without the support of the city government's elected officials, where the school district and city are separate jurisdictions, efforts to implement a locally-initiated desegregation plan could not have succeeded in Seattle.

School Board member Suzanne Hittman made that statement in a report prepared for the National School Board Association's Ad Hoc Committee on Desegregation entitled "Municipal Government/District Cooperation in Desegregation" after the School Board had adopted the Seattle Plan. Seattle's desegregation effort was successful because it was initiated with the support of city government, largely through the efforts of Mayor Wesley Uhlman and the work of the city's Office of Policy Planning (OPP).

Although the boundaries of the Seattle school district and the incorporated city of Seattle are substantially coterminous, the two government entities are separate and autonomous. According to Uhlman:

Seattle is fairly unique in that there is absolutely no formal relationship between city government and the school district. Many larger cities have a very close, not only legal but informal, relationship between the two entities. Until recently in our history, Seattle has never had really any interaction between the two, informally or legally. This creates some enormous problems because what happens to the school district directly impacts and can work in opposition to the objectives of the city. If, for example, the city has as one of its goals the building of a neighborhood, and the school district comes along and takes the neighborhood school out, you have a dichotomy of purposes. This oftentimes creates a rather serious problem in terms of "city building" or "city saving." That was a concern of mine when desegregation was being planned as a citywide effort. The school district had the legal ability, and I suppose even the political ability, to tell me and to tell the city, "This is our problem, and we're going to deal with it irrespective of its effect upon the city." This, however, was not the attitude of the school district during planning for desegregation. Quite the contrary. But the potential existed.[1]

The city and the school district had found themselves on opposite sides of the issue of school closure in 1974. The district was attempting to close some schools because of declining enrollment. City government had not been involved in the planning for school closure and found itself reacting after the fact in opposition to the School Board's plans. Uhlman did not want a repeat of the school closure issue with desegregation planning. As Uhlman put it, with desegregation, "We had to push ourselves up to the table to play poker," to be involved at the front end of discussions on desegregation, rather than to react after a decision had been made.

The subject of public school desegregation was not a new one to Uhlman. Before being elected mayor of Seattle, Uhlman, an attorney, had served in both the House and Senate of the Washington State Legislature. As a member of the legislature, Uhlman proposed an interdistrict desegregation plan in 1967–68. He recalls:

As a member of the state legislature, I proposed a program which would have involved busing, but which was much more important than busing. I proposed that we acquire the Luther Burbank site on Mercer Island. The plan received a great deal of interest and publicity, but no interest at all from Mercer Islanders. It was to be used as an interdistrict strategy for desegregation. We had a major plan all developed. We spent some money. We received some interest from Seattle, but none from Mercer Island; in fact, out-and-out hostility. It was on the front pages of the papers for days.[2]

Mercer Island is in the middle of Lake Washington, east of Seattle across a mile-long floating bridge – a ten-minute drive from Garfield High School in the predominately black inner city.

Mayor Uhlman's two sons had always attended Seattle Public Schools, and both had participated in the voluntary racial transfer program. The mayor's interest in public education in Seattle was both a personal and a professional concern.

Uhlman became aware that the subject of desegregation would be addressed more aggressively through press coverage and from staff members in the Office of Policy Planning in the fall of 1976. In a November memo, OPP informed Uhlman that the possibility existed that a lawsuit could be filed against the School Board, charging that the public schools were illegally segregated. The memo suggested that the mayor meet with representatives of the organizations threatening to sue the district, specifically the Seattle branch of the NAACP and the ACLU of Washington. Attorneys and representatives of these groups met with the mayor and outlined their reasons for considering the suit.

Uhlman also served as a member of the Executive Committee of the United States Conference of Mayors, and met regularly with a small group of mayors from principal cities around the country where he had the opportunity not only to become personally acquainted with other mayors, but to share in discussions with them about their problems and his own. Kevin White, mayor of Boston, was also a member of this small group. Desegregation was a significant problem in Boston. As Uhlman recalls:

One of the problems that had begun to develop was the whole desegregation effort in Boston. It had been particularly explosive, and it really had had a very devastating effect on Kevin White as an individual and as mayor. It also had a devastating effect on his city. The police were daily involved in major kinds of altercations. I came back from one of our meetings feeling very strongly that we should get involved. It was Kevin's feeling and advice that since he and the city and the police department and the city's services were impacted by the schools, that they wished they had had a role in the desegregation planning. So I came back to Seattle fully determined that we would have a role.

When I came back, I called upon the Office of Policy Planning — more specifically upon Woody Wilkinson [then director of OPP], in whom I had a great deal of confidence — to begin to set up the legal mechanism and certainly the informal mechanism for our taking a leadership role.[3]

Uhlman did not want Seattle schools under the control of a federal judge or desegregation "master." According to the mayor:

History shows in other cities where you had some outside entity, other than the community, running the school system, you had a problem. The basic problem is lack of control over the day-to-day decision-making process. If you had a master, someone who is not at all connected with the political processes in the community, someone in whom the city has little or no confidence or faith, problems result.

We have some faith in our own processes when we can go to the polls and elect School Board members who in turn hire the administrators who control our school system. I have no faith at all in a person a federal court judge orders to run our school district. I would have no input, and no involvement, and thus no faith in the process. And I think the public feels that very strongly. We can look at what has happened to other cities where that has occurred, and you have violence and mistrust — you have all of the things that go toward destroying a school system.[4]

Mayor Uhlman was convinced that a threatened lawsuit could ultimately be filed and that some illegal segregation could be proven in Seattle. This opinion came from conversations with the NAACP and the ACLU, but also from evidence gathered by the city's legal department, and the opinion of an outside consultant brought in by OPP. The school district's legal counsel did not dispute the opinion.

Before deciding to do anything about possible desegregation efforts, Uhlman wanted to gather information. In order to determine what his best approach to desegregation would be, Uhlman asked the OPP to research two areas: first, to survey mayors in other school districts to determine what their experiences had been; and second, to develop some projections on what desegregation could do to the city's tax base as the result of the much-discussed white or middle-class flight which can accompany desegregation efforts.

To accomplish the first goal, staff members in the OPP conducted telephone interviews with the equivalent of a "deputy mayor" in twenty-five major cities across the country which had experienced desegregation. The questionnaire which was developed asked for information both about the public position and activities of the mayors and about the mayors' personal feelings. Each city had either been desegregated by court order or by a requirement of the HEW. The survey gathered information on the relationship between city government and the school district, the relationship between the boundaries of the district and municipality, the size of the district, the racial composition of the city and district, the source of the desegregation plan, the specifics of the plan, the city's posture on desegregation, and the ramifications and changes which resulted in these cities from desegregation. The survey also attempted to discover the amount of information city officials had about the school district. On the whole, the city officials surveyed knew relatively little about their school districts. With the exception of information obtained in the survey concerning the mayors' private (as opposed to public) response to desegregation, the survey was made public. Of other city mayors' personal feelings regarding desegregation, Uhlman says:

The mayors said that it is very politically risky to take a leadership role in desegregation because you do alienate a number of persons. Any time you are discussing desegregation, you are going to alienate a certain number of people in white neighborhoods – places where individuals have moved to escape these kinds of problems. To these people, the solution to the problem [of segregation] is to be left alone.

However, my principal feelings, regardless of the political implications, were that we just had to do something. We just had to get involved and take that kind of risk.[5]

The research on white and middle-class flight was based on a model developed by James Colman[1] which compared the white and black populations in a small northern city. At the suggestion of Shelly Yapp, liaison to the school district from the city, the Colman model was modified by OPP to be used as a predictive tool, something that had not been done elsewhere.

The research indicated that Seattle could expect to experience little white and middle-class flight, with all of it taking place during the first two years of the plan's implementation.

In a February 8 memo to Mayor Uhlman, R.W. (Woody) Wilkinson, Jr., director of OPP, outlined the expected impacts on Seattle of school desegregation. In part, the memo reads:

In an earlier survey of 25 cities made by OPP, slightly more than half of the cities indicate that their school system had experienced a decline in White enrollment since desegregation; however, a number of those cities were unable to distinguish whether the loss was simply a continuation of the existing trend or an acceleration of the trend due to desegregation. Ten of the cities interviewed said that desegregation had been accompanied by an increase in private school enrollment, and in seven cities, new private schools opened. A number of these cities, however, suggested that over two or three years, the public schools had regained many of the students that had initially left for private schools.

All the researchers do agree that to the extent that desegregation has an impact on White flight, it is larger in the south than in the north. Moreover, there seems to be unanimous agreement that the proportion Black students represent in the enrollment is an important variable, and that those cities with a high proportion of Blacks have experienced higher rates of White flight in the presence of desegregation than those cities with a smaller Black population . . . .

The impact on the White population occurs in the same year as desegregation and is a one-time phenomenon. Desegregation does not appear to lead to a progressive acceleration in the rate of White outmigration.[6]

After delineating these and other findings, the February 8 memo to the mayor concluded:

The most we can predict for Seattle is a one-time, one percent loss of White enrollment, to take place during the first year of the desegregation program. The least we can predict is no effect. In other words, although there is wide disagreement over whether or not desegregation causes White flight, the predicted results for Seattle are much the same. Desegregation of the public schools may have no impact on Seattle or, at the other extreme, the impact will be small and relatively short-term.[7]

Because of the disagreement among experts on the subject of white flight, the city always viewed this research as tentative.

By early February, then, Mayor Uhlman had the information he needed to develop a position on desegregation. The position that the mayor took was basically that the school district should initiate desegregation, rather than permit the issue to become the basis for a legal battle which could result in a court-ordered plan for Seattle that would take control of the public schools out of the hands of the locally elected School Board and, as a result, the local community.

Uhlman also realized that if this was to be accomplished, Seattle needed a desegregation plan that was mandatory in nature. A voluntary approach to student transfers would not accomplish the goal of desegregation and, furthermore, would not satisfy the groups which were considering suing the district. Publicly, Uhlman felt he could say that Seattle should desegregate schools itself, rather than wait for a court order, but politically he could not say that the desegregation plan must be mandatory.

Simultaneously, the superintendent and School Board were in the process of developing a voluntary approach to desegregation, the Magnet Plan. This plan was discussed from January 1977 on, and was unanimously adopted by the School Board on March 7, 1977. The school district's decision to continue to attempt to desegregate schools with only voluntary student transfer strategies precipitated an increase in the level of activity and support for a lawsuit to bring about desegregation. Seattle Public Schools were becoming increasingly segregated, and the voluntary racial transfer program, initiated in 1963, had had little effect on ending segregation.

After the School Board adopted the Magnet Plan, Mayor Uhlman called Superintendent Moberly and invited him to a meeting in the mayor's office. Woody Wilkinson from OPP was present, and Olaf Kvamme, director of Intergovernmental Relations for the school district, also attended. Uhlman told Moberly that he wanted the decision to desegregate Seattle Public Schools to be made locally and that, to be successful, a desegregation plan must be mandatory. Moberly told the mayor that if the school district was going to embark on a mandatory desegregation effort, it would need a public demonstration of sufficient community support for such an effort. Moberly remembers this conversation and others with Uhlman:

What I told Wes very early was that you can't expect that the School Board will make that kind of decision, or that a superintendent will get out on a limb unless there is strong support from the leadership in the city. If that leadership isn't there, you can't sit back and blame the Board for doing nothing. "You've got a responsibility," I said to Wes.

Wes knew the problems of an elected Board. I told him that without the Chamber of Commerce's support for desegregation, we were going to have some real problems. We still had to pass the levy and needed their support for that.[8]

During the time desegregation was being seriously discussed, prior to the adoption of the Seattle Plan and the end of Uhlman's tenure as mayor of Seattle (December 1977), Moberly and Uhlman had several conversations about desegregation. Both describe their relationship as a good one. In Uhlman's words:

Moberly and I had some formal and informal discussions at various functions. We've been good friends — not close friends, but good friends — over the years, and this developed out of the basis of some real respect for each other. Moberly was very receptive to the city's involvement in desegregation. He felt almost as beleaguered in his job as I did in mine. Maybe there is some comfort in commiserating on mutual problems.[9]

The fact that good lines of communication, based on mutual respect, existed between the superintendent and the mayor helped bring about the Seattle Plan.

Moberly, however, was not entirely convinced that Uhlman supported a district-initiated mandatory desegregation plan after the first formal meeting called by Uhlman. During a subsequent public hearing on the Magnet Plan, Shelly Yapp, liaison to the district, made a statement on behalf of the city, with the concurrence of Woody Wilkinson and Mayor Uhlman. In the statement, Yapp indicated that the city felt that the Magnet Plan was not sufficient to keep the school district out of court. While the superintendent had heard the same thing from Uhlman personally, he was not prepared to hear the city make a public statement encouraging the district to take more aggressive steps to end segregation. Moberly questioned Yapp's authority to make the public statement at the School Board meeting. Recalling this incident Uhlman says:

I remember Moberly saying he felt, and I agreed with him, that we really ought to be working more and more closely so that we were together in public. At that point in time he had not yet fully realized that we were there in a supportive role.

From the outset Moberly welcomed us, which is not the case in some other cities where there are feelings of "turf."[10]

Moberly, however, also knew that he had pressure from city government to contend with to keep the school district out of court.

Wes Uhlman was not seeking a third term as mayor of Seattle, and several City Council positions were also up for election in November 1977.[11] As campaigns were beginning in early spring of 1977, Uhlman asked Shelly Yapp from OPP to meet with each of the candidates for City Council, and the City Council members who were seeking to replace Uhlman as mayor, to ask that they allow the mayor to speak for the city on the subject of desegregation and not use the issue as a platform in the election. All council members and candidates agreed. Though candidates were questioned by voters during the campaign about desegregation, all deferred to the mayor, and stated simply that they would support the law of the land. The mayor's leadership also provided an opportunity for candidates to avoid having to address this extremely controversial subject.[12]

Shortly after the first of the year (1977) Uhlman also briefed city department heads, expressing his personal support for the school district's developing its own desegregation plan rather than waiting for a court to order Seattle's schools desegregated. Included in the briefing of department heads was a presentation by William Maynard, the school district's desegregation director. Maynard explained that it was becoming increasingly apparent that Seattle's voluntary desegregation plan was not going to eliminate enough segregation to avoid the threatened lawsuit. Insufficient student transfers to and from racially segregated schools were taking place.

A tangible method of demonstrating the necessary support for desegregation efforts was needed if the superintendent and the School Board were going to address citywide desegregation with an effective, and therefore mandatory, desegregation plan. The vehicle used was a joint letter signed by Mayor Uhlman and the presidents of the Chamber of Commerce, the Municipal League, and the Seattle Urban League.

Uhlman had been cultivating the Chamber of Commerce and the business community's support for desegregation efforts informally. He describes that process:

The Chamber of Commerce, for the past several years, has been under very progressive leadership, as opposed to the first several years of my administration, with the arrival, for example, of George Duff as the chamber's chief executive. He has a quiet and a very positive influence on the chamber's role in some central issues. I felt it was very wise, and would be successful to approach the chamber and involve them intricately in a leadership role on desegregation. There was some resistance in the chamber, as there would be in any organization with such a diverse membership, but we decided that if we were really going to be successful [in obtaining a locally controlled desegregation plan], we had to have a very broad base of support, particularly from the business community.

I had several discussions at the Rainier Club, and at Chamber of Commerce parties and meetings [about the need for desegregation]. The litany that I was preaching was that they had a stake, a business and economic stake, in this community, and if they wanted to protect that, they were going to have to solve the school desegregation issue.

I told them, "If we don't do anything, if you don't get involved, we can expect destruction of property." Fear is as great a motivator as goodness and kindness. All we had to do was look on the national television news and see what happens in other cities when the issue does not get solved through leadership. That's what leadership is all about — staying out ahead of the curve, trying to anticipate the problems and somehow or another alleviate those problems. In some instances we appealed to their best interests; in some instances we appealed to their economic interests.[13]

The superintendent and School Board president and businessman Don Olson were especially clear about the need for the involvement of the business community in efforts to end segregation in Seattle. They felt desegregation could not happen without support from the Chamber of Commerce.

The suggestion for the joint letter probably was made by Olaf Kvamme in a conversation with Shelly Yapp. Yapp believes that Don Olson probably made the suggestion to Kvamme, who had participated in the discussions between Uhlman and Moberly.[14] Uhlman's immediate response was to suggest that he sign the letter along with two friends, Wallace Bunn and Mark Cooper. Ultimately this idea evolved into the joint letter signed by the presidents of the Chamber of Commerce, the Municipal League and the Seattle Urban League. Bunn, president-elect of the Chamber of Commerce and chief executive officer of Pacific Northwest Bell, did not sign the May 20 letter, but did sign other subsequent joint communications. Mark Cooper, a Safeco Insurance Company executive, was serving that year as the president of the board of the Seattle Urban League. Both were respected businessmen. The reasons for including the Municipal League and Urban League in the letter, according to Uhlman, were:

The Municipal League was asked because they have been around a long time, even though they have been waning greatly in their influence lately. Nevertheless, they have been respected because of their past laurels, their past accomplishments. The Urban League was an integral part of this because of Jerry Page's presence and because of their ongoing role in desegregation efforts. They were the catalyst, the burr under the saddle of the school district.[15]

The May 20 letter urged the School Board to develop a definition of racial isolation (segregation) and to set a deadline for eliminating it.

The City of Seattle, the Seattle Chamber of Commerce, the Municipal League of Seattle and King County, and the Seattle Urban League wish to go on record together and as one voice to declare united support for your adoption of a definition of racial isolation and measurable goals leading to the elimination of racial isolation in the Seattle Public Schools, prior to court-ordered and mandated desegregation remedy.[16]

The ACLU had met with Mayor Uhlman, and the mayor knew what the district must do to forestall a lawsuit — that is, define racial isolation and set a deadline for eliminating it. As Uhlman said, "Our 'voluntary' desegregation plan was adopted at the point of a gun."[17] The "gun" was the threat of a lawsuit.

The May 20 joint letter is significant, not only because it provided the needed encouragement for the School Board to take action to desegregate schools by its own action, but because it is an excellent example of cooperation among four entities in the city of Seattle which had never before written a joint letter. The process of drafting the letter was carried out by the staffs of the four organizations involved, and according to Shelly Yapp, "Every word was reviewed, probably thirty times."[18] The process was completed in about two weeks — an incredible feat.

CHAPTER 9

THE LETTER

The Senders

The Seattle Chamber of Commerce and the Municipal League of Seattle and King County were active participants in the decision to desegregate Seattle Public Schools. They became involved in the issue partly because of their ties to Superintendent David Moberly.

The school superintendents who preceded David Moberly in Seattle were not held in high regard by the Chamber of Commerce and the business community in general because of their approach (or lack of approach) to fiscal management. It is probably not coincidental that Seattle's only double levy failure in recent years (funds from property taxes levied by the School Board could be submitted to the voters twice for approval) occurred in 1975, the year the Chamber of Commerce opposed the levy. During the process of hiring a new superintendent, the Chamber of Commerce worked with School Board member Don Olson to insure that the district found someone who (in the words of Board member Patt Sutton) "spoke 'budget' fluently and without accent."[1] David Moberly fit the job description, and the Chamber of Commerce was pleased that the new superintendent could discuss the management of the district in terms of sound traditional business practices. Early in his administration Moberly spent a considerable amount of time cultivating a relationship with the Chamber of Commerce. The superintendent saw the chamber as his best source of political strength in the city and fulfilled the School Board's directive to pass the upcoming levy by insuring that the chamber would endorse it. Because the Chamber of Commerce had played a significant role in hiring Superintendent Moberly, they would, therefore have a tendency to support his administration.

The Municipal League of Seattle and King County is a respected nonpartisan civic organization, concerned mainly with good government in the area. Municipal League members generally shared the opinion that the

Seattle Public Schools needed a better manager when Superintendent Moberly was hired. They too were pleased with the choice.

In Seattle, the Chamber of Commerce and the Municipal League not only supported desegregation, but assisted the School Board in making the decision to desegregate schools by their own action, rather than fight a court battle. While minority and civil rights groups can be expected to support desegregation efforts, the involvement of the Seattle Chamber of Commerce and the Municipal League meant that much of the divisiveness and turmoil which can accompany desegregation was avoided in Seattle.

> Across the nation in the various school districts included in the Commission [on Civil Rights] study, where officials and community leaders have given their support, the process of desegregating the schools has tended to go relatively smoothly. In these districts the community at large more readily accepted desegregation. Where civic leaders publicly opposed desegregation, however, they provided sanction to its opponents, who believe they have been given license to disobey the law and disrupt the community and its schools in protest.[2]

Involvement of members of the Chamber of Commerce and the Municipal League also guaranteed that the point of view of civic and business leaders in Seattle was well represented in the kind of plan Seattle would adopt.

Both the chamber and the Municipal League had active education committees prior to 1977 when discussions about desegregation became intense. These committees had generally concerned themselves with issues such as school financing, the district's budget, staff accountability and improving the academic performance of students in Seattle. In response to renewed activity on the subject of desegregation, the Chamber of Commerce formed a special Desegregation Task Force in the winter of 1976.[3] The task force was chaired by Russ Amick, a local businessman. The Municipal League discussed desegregation through its existing Education Committee, chaired by Eben Carlson, a local attorney. There was some overlap between the membership of the Desegregation Task Force of the chamber and the Education Committee of the Municipal League, and good communication links existed between the two bodies.

C. Mike Berry, president of Seattle First National Bank, was president of the Chamber of Commerce in the spring of 1977; Wallace R. Bunn became president later that year. Bunn was then president of Pacific Northwest Bell. Mark Cooper, a local Safeco Insurance Company executive, was vice-president of the chamber's Desegregation Task Force and was as well chairman of the board of the Seattle Urban League during 1977. J. Shan Mullin, a local corporate attorney, became president of the board of the Municipal League in May, 1976, a position he held for two years. Mullin was also a member of the chamber's Desegregation Task Force. All of these individuals are political moderates. Of the above, Shan Mullin was probably the most extensively involved in the day-to-day process of deciding on a desegregation plan for Seattle.

Shan Mullin initially became informed about the urgency of addressing desegregation in Seattle through a series of forums conducted by the People Power Coalition in the spring of 1977. In April, increased activity on the part of a number of civil rights groups was taking place, aimed at bringing about the end to segregation in Seattle through a lawsuit.

Shan Mullin had begun to contact members of the community organizations who were considering suing the district in April to ask that they postpone a suit to give groups like the Municipal League time to "catch up." Mullin promised to support efforts to end segregation. He felt that the School Board could be persuaded to address the issue itself and that a lawsuit would therefore be unnecessary. He recalls the period:

There was a fair amount of activity at that time on the subject of desegregation. I remember attending several forums at the YMCA held by People Power. I had also been asked by the chamber to serve on their Desegregation Task Force. I became more and more concerned about what I called a deterioration in the whole situation. By that I mean that we were heading for a confrontation, probably in court. That was causing me to grow more and more concerned about the consequences of that approach to the problem, as opposed to trying to find our own solution. I felt that we should not assume that the only way to desegregate was to have the school district fight it out in court.[4]

According to Russ Amick, chair of the chamber's Desegregation Task Force, the chamber was kept informed on desegregation activities by then Board president Don Olson, in the same manner Olson had communicated with the chamber during the hiring of Superintendent Moberly. Amick recalls that during the discussions regarding hiring the new superintendent, desegregation was also addressed, primarily in terms of voluntary student transfers and magnet programs. Don Olson had attended the equivalent of a magnet program during high school and favored this approach to desegregation when Moberly was hired.

In the winter of 1976 the chamber's task force, composed of board-level members of the chamber, had become informed on the proposed Magnet Plan and had endorsed this approach to desegregation. The Municipal League also endorsed the Magnet Plan, unlike most of the community organizations which had been discussing the desegregation at meetings of the District-Wide Advisory Committee on Desegregation. A January 21 first draft of a Municipal League resolution on voluntary desegregation reveals the opinion of league members at that time. One part of the statement reads:

A voluntary desegregation plan is preferable and could bring the community together in a common effort; a mandatory plan could tear it apart . . . .

and:

The Municipal League supports the efforts of the School Board to effect a voluntary desegregation plan.[5]

The Chamber of Commerce had endorsed the Magnet Plan on March 29, "for a variety of reasons, not the least of which is the voluntary aspect."[6]

When the possibility of a lawsuit became increasingly likely, the chamber's Desegregation Task Force discussed the legal vulnerability of the district informally with Superintendent Moberly and Board president Don Olson. Russ Amick recalls Olson telling him that legal counsel for the Board had indicated that in a couple of instances it was likely that acts of illegal segregation would be proven. It was the stated opinion of the Board's legal counsel that in these situations, "It was an open and shut case."[7] As Amick recalls, specific actions of the Board which might be considered proof of illegal segregation were discussed. One instance mentioned was the difference in the way students were assigned when schools were closed. When predominately black Horace Mann Elementary School was closed, black students were assigned to distant predominately white schools; however, when predominately white Interlake Elementary School was closed, its student body was reassigned to adjacent white schools. Because the chamber had been fighting with the school district for years on the issues of poor management and fiscal accountability, it seemed possible that the Seattle Public Schools had also been negligent and caused some segregation, according to Amick.[8] Seeing that a lawsuit was imminent, the Chamber felt that the school district would probably be found guilty of some illegal segregation. They did not want Seattle to come under court order which would allow a federal judge to run the district.[9]

The State of Washington had been found guilty of violating Indian fishing treaty rights by Federal Judge George Boldt, and Boldt, in essence, was in control of the state's fishing industry. The chamber did not want a similar situation to develop in the public schools. Many members of the chamber felt that court-ordered segregation plans were undesirable, having seen national press coverage of court-ordered efforts in cities such as Boston, where civil disruption had taken place.[10]

Mayor Wes Uhlman had decided by January 1977 that he preferred that the School Board end segregation by its own action, rather than allow a federal court to order desegregation.[11] And by April of that year some members of the School Board were becomingly increasingly aware that they would have to act quickly if they were to avoid being sued.

Uhlman believed that the School Board probably could be persuaded to take action to end segregation if there was sufficient support from business and civic leaders in Seattle for that action. The idea of demonstrating the needed community support through a letter to the School Board was probably initially proposed to the other signatories by Uhlman.

The chamber agreed to sign the letter because it felt that it was necessary to correct any illegal segregation. Chamber members saw the joint letter as a way of helping Superintendent Moberly by keeping him out of court. Because no illegal segregation would have to be proven if a court battle was avoided, the question of guilt would become moot.[12]

Mayor Uhlman asked the staff of the city's Office of Policy Planning to contact Mike Berry, Mark Cooper and Shan Mullin to be joint signatories to the letter.[13] Coincidentally, these individuals were the presidents of the boards of the Chamber of Commerce, the Municipal League and the Seattle Urban League.

The Municipal League developed the idea of encouraging the School Board to take action which would avoid a lawsuit by its own internal process. Municipal League members were not responding to a request from city government when they agreed to sign the letter. They were already in the process of developing support from established leadership to take the action necessary to avoid the lawsuit.[14]

One individual who participated in discussions concerning this subject with members of both the Municipal League and the Chamber of Commerce was Jerry Skutt. Skutt joined the Education Committee of the Municipal League and the Desegregation Task Force of the Chamber of Commerce in early

1977 and was appointed as the Municipal League's representative to DWAC the summer of 1977.[15] He participated in meetings in which the NAACP and the ACLU discussed their proposed suit against the school district during April 1977. Recalling the total process for developing the idea of the joint letter, Skutt says:

I had an interest in the subject of desegregation because of my strong feelings about the quality of education in this city. I had great apprehensions about the cloud hanging over our heads with the filing of a suit and the two or three years' time period it might take to resolve such a suit. I felt there would be a detrimental effect, not only on the quality of education, but on people's perception of the city.

I began attending meetings of the chamber's desegregation committee in the month of April 1977, and attended several in May. One meeting was with NAACP representatives including Lacy Steele and Connie Herring. Another meeting was with the ACLU, whose representatives included David Harrison and Fred Noland, their attorney. We began to sense that we were really not as far apart as had been previously thought, at least not with the NAACP. The chamber members at those meetings included Russ Amick, Mark Cooper, Shan Mullin, Robert Thompson, publisher of the *Seattle Post-Intelligencer,* and Ancil Payne, president of KING Broadcasting.[16]

At the meeting with the NAACP, I stressed that we were dealing with seven very politically vulnerable School Board members who would really have their necks out were they to take the issue [of desegregation] on. We had to convey to them not only that desegregation needed to be addressed, but that as organizations we would stand behind their efforts. Russ Amick wanted to check with Don Olson before doing anything publicly. He talked to Don and got a very favorable response.

On May 9 several of us got together for a breakfast meeting at the University Towers Hotel. As I recall, those there included: from the Municipal League, Shan Mullin, Eben Carlson and myself; from the chamber, Russ Amick, Mark Cooper and the chamber staff member.[17] The meeting included a discussion about what other organizations ought to be approached to join a coalition to call on the School Board to address desegregation.

At the same time, discussions were going on within the Municipal League as to how best the concerned organizations could jointly declare their support for [the needed] School Board action. We believed that the league, chamber and perhaps others would join such a coalition. Further, we felt that Uhlman would, under reasonable circumstances, step forward as part of the group. While consideration was given to a media event, such as a news conference, it was concluded that a joint letter was the best way to go.[18]

Shortly after moving to Seattle, Rob Makin, a native of Chicago via Washington, D.C., joined the staff of the Chamber of Commerce in February 1977 as staff to the Education Committee and the Desegregation Task Force. His first responsibility was to work on the second levy campaign that year. His second assignment was to assist with drafting the joint letter. He recalls that Sidney Freeman of the city's Office of Policy Planning wrote the first draft. Makin's calendar records that his first discussion with Freeman about the letter took place on May 12. Freeman had called Makin, introduced herself because the two had never met, and arranged for a meeting, at which they worked on the first revision of the letter.[19] Later Jerry Skutt, Shan Mullin and Jerome Page, executive director of the Urban League, also worked on revising drafts. The letter went through numerous rewrites between May 12 and May 20. Negotiations concerning the content of the letter were handled by the staff members of the four bodies. some of whom had not previously known each other. There was no precedent for such a joint letter. Each draft was then reviewed by Uhlman, Berry, Mullin and Cooper, with Freeman and Makin doing much of the negotiating to gain approval for the revisions. The four bodies were able to agree on the content of the letter in a matter of about ten days, an incredible feat. The content was approved by the Executive Committee of the Municipal League and the Desegregation Task Force and Executive Committee of the chamber before being sent to the School Board. Although the letter is dated May 20, it did not arrive at the school district offices until the twenty-fifth, probably because it was not approved until that date. The impending lawsuit was the pressure which provided the incentive for these four organizations to accomplish this joint effort, unparalleled by any previous or subsequent action. The letter reads, in part:

Experience elsewhere indicates that a commitment on the part of local leadership has contributed immeasurably to successful desegregation of the public schools. As civic leaders, we have expressed support for desegregation to you individually in the past and will continue to do so in the future. Now, however, the City of Seattle, the Seattle Chamber of Commerce, the Municipal League of Seattle and King County, and the Seattle Urban League wish to go on record together and as one voice to declare united support for your adoption of a definition of racial isolation and measurable goals leading to the elimination of racial isolation in the Seattle Public Schools, prior to a Court-ordered and mandated desegregation remedy.[20]

The letter went on to state that the signatories believed that "an integrated education offers children a chance to share self-knowledge and learning experiences"[21] to adjust to a pluralistic society, and pointed out that Seattle should not expect to experience significant middle-class migration as a result of desegregation as long as the School Board maintained its commitment, as long as there was citizen involvement, and as long as support from civic leadership for desegregation was maintained.

The letter was clearly a turning point in desegregation efforts in Seattle. Don Olson felt obliged to do what the letter urged him to do, guaranteeing that at least four Board members (a majority of the seven members) would vote in favor of a definition and timetable. Cheryl Bleakney had introduced a resolution the week before the letter arrived (May 11) asking the Board to take the same action urged by the letter. Suzanne Hittman and Dorothy Hollingsworth could be counted on to support desegregation efforts.

A definition of racial imbalance and a timetable to eliminate it could be expected to prevent a lawsuit, or if one were filed, to prevent an early court date for the case. No suit was filed.

Not everybody involved in writing, approving and signing the joint letter saw the Seattle Plan as a likely outcome of their action. Some probably were hoping for a plan that relied on strictly voluntary methods to move students; some expected that voluntary efforts would have a mandatory backup. It is likely that only Jerome Page of the Urban League expected (or at least hoped) that the Urban League's Triad Plan would become the basis of Seattle's comprehensive desegregation plan.

Reflecting on this period, Russ Amick feels that the chamber probably guessed that the letter would result in a strictly voluntary desegregation plan that would work. It was Amick's impression that Moberly still thought that the district could desegregate with voluntary student transfer strategies when the letter arrived in May, and that Mayor Uhlman,[22] Shan Mullin, and Mark Cooper believed the final Seattle Plan would be voluntary.[23]

Amick is a resident of the Laurelhurst Elementary attendance area, which participated in the middle school desegregation effort. In 1977 enough voluntary racial transfer students were recruited from the Laurelhurst area to fill that area's quota, and no mandatory assignments were necessary. However, mandatory assignments were needed to fill Laurelhurst's quota in other years, and were needed from the twenty or so other elementary attendance areas each year the Middle School Plan was in operation. Reflecting on this phenomenon, Amick feels that Laurelhurst was successful in recruiting voluntary racial transfer students for two reasons: first, because of the presence of the mandatory backup, and second, because Laurelhurst residents perceived Meany Middle School (to which students transferred) to be superior in educational quality to their neighborhood middle school (Eckstein). However, at the time the May 20 letter was sent, Amick guessed that a voluntary desegregation plan could be written to desegregate Seattle's schools without the need for mandatory busing, and that this was the likely outcome of the chamber's pressure on the Board to take action to end segregation.[24]

Jerry Skutt basically agrees with Amick. He saw the intent of the joint letter as an effort to avoid a possible lawsuit. Regarding the kind of desegregation plan that would result, he recalls:

In no case, to my knowledge, did we discuss the how-tos [how to desegregate], though everybody expected it would be some extension of the current magnet program but not much tougher. We were simply interested in getting on with it.[25]

The Magnet Plan relied solely on voluntary student transfers.

At least some members of the Municipal League and Chamber of Commerce saw their involvement in the joint letter as an effort to prevent a lawsuit. They responded to the immediacy of the lawsuit by asking that the School Board *eliminate* racial isolation without necessarily expecting that this would require mandatory student transfers.

Other individuals involved in the two organizations expected that some mandatory student assignment would be needed to eliminate racial isolation. Rob Makin understood that the desegregation plan would need a mandatory component if the School Board followed through on the requests in the May 20 letter. He also believes that Wallace Bunn, the new president of the Chamber of Commerce, understood the mandatory implications of the joint letter.[26] Both Shan Mullin[27] and Eben Carlson[28] believed that some element of mandatory desegregation would probably be included in the final plan. Mullin anticipated the possibility of a mandatory backup to voluntary recruitment such as that in operation in the Middle School Plan. This was probably the most common assumption about the nature of a final comprehensive desegregation plan, shared by a great many individuals close to the process in May of 1977.

The Receivers

In the spring of 1977, School Board members had also been wrestling seriously with the need for further desegregation. To determine what the administration needed from the Board to write a comprehensive desegregation plan, shortly after the Board adopted the Magnet Plan in March, Suzanne Hittman met with Dick Dyksterhuis, second-in-command in the district's desegregation office. As she recalls:

> I said, "Okay, now if we really want to desegregate the school district, what do you need to know?" Dick's response was, "Number one, I need to know what it is you want to achieve. Number two, I need to know if there are any strategies I cannot use. Then let me loose and give me a deadline." So that was the task of the next two months.[29]

In March probably only two of the seven School Board members would have voted in favor of a desegregation plan that employed mandatory student transfer strategies – Suzanne Hittman and Dorothy Hollingsworth. A third Board member became active in May.

Cheryl Bleakney began to take definite action to assist the School Board to decide whether it was going to allow a lawsuit to take place or was going to take the initiative in desegregation efforts, by calling for a definition of racial imbalance and a timetable to eliminate it. As she recalls:

> It was May 1977. We had another legal session [a closed-door Board meeting to discuss legal questions]. Suzanne and I kept insisting on legal sessions because we could hear what the NAACP, the ACLU and the Church Council were saying. We kept insisting that we talk about what we were going to do because we were inexorably moving toward this lawsuit. I just wanted us to go into it having decided whether we wanted to or not. That was what was making me so mad.
>
> After that legal session, Suzanne and I went out for a drink. We talked about various strategies, and I said I was going to the newspapers with a proposal. I stayed up all night writing it, and I called her in the morning and read her what I had written. Then I called Mary Elayne Dunphy [*Seattle Times* reporter]. I told her I would bring her a copy so she could make that night's paper. I knew what I was doing and I was scared stiff.
>
> When I read it to Eric Nalder [*Seattle Post-Intelligencer* reporter], he said, "That's kind of weak." And I said, "Oh, no! All hell's going to break loose!" And he called me the next day and said, "You were right."

I should have notified Don [Olson, president of the School Board] of what I had done. I read it to Moberly. When I told Carmela Bowns [legal counsel] what I was doing, she tried to counsel me, saying, "Do you realize that if you set a definition you will have to comply with it?"

I was calling for a definition and a timetable. We had a Board meeting the next day [May 11], and I said I was prepared to offer a motion that day that would set a definition for segregation and set a time certain for ending it. It was zero hour. If we hadn't done it then, we would have been in court. That was really it.[30]

The School Board meeting on May 11 was a heated one. Bleakney made her motion, and it was tabled. Uncomfortable with open controversy, Board president Don Olson was very upset by the Board meeting and wrote an "open letter" to the Board, charging members with being overly emotional. The letter was published in the newspaper before reaching the Board.

Earlier, at a meeting of the Board's Desegregation Committee in mid-April, Sidney Freeman from the city had begun to realize that the members of the committee were trying to move the School Board to do something more decisive about desegregation. She communicated this fact to Shelly Yapp, who made an appointment to have lunch with Cheryl Bleakney. Yapp offered the city's help if the Board should need it. Bleakney recalls:

Shelly asked me to have lunch with her and she was sort of dancing around the subject for a while, indicating that she agreed with what I was doing, and indicated that there would be some help from the mayor's office if we were to push for desegregation. I knew that the mayor didn't want us to go to court through Arlis's [Stewart, director of the People Power Coalition, who kept Bleakney informed of what was happening in the community from about January 1977 on] communication, but I'd never had any direct communication.[31]

After her motion of May 11 was tabled, Bleakney asked for help, realizing that Don Olson was upset by the May 11 discussion, as demonstrated by his open letter to the Board.

At that point I called Shelly and said, "You said there might be some help and I'm calling in that promise. I'm asking for help." Shelly told me about the letter at that point. The letter was amazing to me because I didn't think they could get it together. Obviously the groundwork had been laid for a long time.[32]

It was Don Olson's vote that produced the majority. He recalls:

I think we could have handled the whole thing [desegregation] if we hadn't had the threat of the lawsuit, which then caused the writing of that letter, which caused me to change my vote. Some of the signatories of that letter didn't fully understand what they were asking for in terms of the effect it would have on me as one of the seven members of the Board.

If we hadn't had the threat of a lawsuit, I think we could have worked this thing out and ended up with essentially what we have now, but we wouldn't have had some of the trauma that we have now.

I tried to get rid of the terms "mandatory" and "voluntary" because they were inflammatory terms. Let's just talk about desegregation, and if we have to have mandatory, I was prepared to take that on in the courts. What I felt we could do is to have a plan in place that would be good enough that it would be defensible in the courts, and that we could term it "voluntary." We could have essentially what we have now and call it voluntary.

With the Magnet Plan we could have been so far down the road toward desegregation that we'd be able to go to court with a plan that had already accomplished quite a bit. As far as I was concerned we were still moving in the right direction at a pretty good pace.

That's when the letter came. Here's a letter signed by some of the more conservative people in town, namely the Municipal League and the Chamber of Commerce. They're not claiming to be liberals by any definition. Here we have these two organizations saying "Do more." So we were being pushed at that point. I wasn't going to take them on and say, "You're wrong, and I'm right.[33]

As Superintendent Moberly viewed the situation:

Back in those days [before the letter], I still thought we were going to be court-ordered to desegregate, realizing that I worked for an elected Board. Elected boards across the country have always left this hot potato for the federal court. At that time I still thought it was going to go to court, and it would have if it hadn't been for the letter signed by the four organizations. That's what swung the vote, or otherwise we would have been in federal court. I know that. We would have been in federal court by a three-to-four vote. They would have voted for a voluntary-only plan which would have resulted in a suit. It [the letter] was a very important thing. It influenced Don Olson, and Olson, in turn, influenced other members of the Board. It surprised me. Elected officials usually don't want to do this sort of thing.[34]

The June 8 School Board resolutions (Board Resolutions 1977–8 and 1977–9), which defined racial imbalance (segregation), set a timetable for eliminating it, and defined the strategies which were appropriate to use, were the decision to eliminate segregation in Seattle. Given the level of community support for their implementation, it was unlikely that the Board would fail to follow through, as they had failed to do with phases two and three following the desegregation of middle schools.

Resolution 1977–8 begins:

WHEREAS, the Board of Directors of Seattle School District No. 1 has found that the best interests of the children of Seattle School District No. 1 will be served by providing all school children with the opportunity for a quality multi-racial education; . . . .

and:

WHEREAS, the Board of Directors is cognizant and appreciative of the strong and united community support for the above described efforts; . . . .

and continues to resolve that racial imbalance would be *eliminated* by the beginning of the 1979–80 school year, "by the use of educationally sound strategies," that half of that segregation would be eliminated in the 1978–79 school year, and that racial imbalance

is defined as the situation that exists when the combined minority student enrollment in a school exceeds the District-Wide combined minority average by 20 percentage points, provided that the single minority enrollment (as defined by current federal categories)[35] of no school will exceed 50 percent of the student body.[36]

Board Resolution 1977–9 described the planning process to be used, identified specific deadlines, and described the strategies which could be used. A structure and timetable for developing various plans to be considered would be brought to the Board for adoption by July. Plans would include already existing desegregation efforts in use in the district. Additional strategies could include facility closures, boundary realignments, pairing, clustering, and zoning; random reassignment by computer could be used in conjunction with educationally sound strategies. The resolution made it clear that virtually all desegregation strategies could be considered. Alternative plans to be reviewed by the Board and the public were to be completed by October 1, 1977, and by December 15, 1977, the Board would select the comprehensive plan.

Several issues were resolved by the passage of these resolutions: specifically, the decision to eliminate racial imbalance, the definition of racial imbalance and the extent to which the community was, had been, and would continue to be involved in the desegregation process.

Seattle had been "working toward" the elimination of racial imbalance for a number of years, while the number of segregated schools in the district increased. Board members discussed whether or not they would commit themselves to the elimination of segregation, a much more difficult task. Dorothy Hollingsworth played a key role in convincing Board members that the time had come to eliminate segregation. As she recalls:

One thing I was sure of – it was time to talk of the elimination of segregation. I was tired. I had spent thirteen years working for it [desegregation], and that's why I really had problems with the Board. There were those who were willing to "work toward the elimination of segregation." And I said, "No!" If someone has their foot on my neck, holding me down, I don't want that foot off a little bit. I want it off all the way.[37]

The definition of racial imbalance was a more complicated issue. Several definitions existed. The State of Washington defined segregation as that situation which exists when the population of a school building includes forty percent or more of a single racial minority group. Emergency School Aid Act guidelines (for federal desegregation funds) define racial imbalance as the situation which exists when the combined racial minority percentage in a single school exceeds fifty percent. The school district had used the Washington State guideline when desegregating middle schools. At that time, desegregation was taking place in a biracial setting. Prior to 1972, Meany Middle School was a black segregated school. By contrast, the Seattle Plan was going to also desegregate schools which had both large Asian American and large black populations, and some which also contained some Hispanic and Native American students. Many members of these various racial minority communities objected to being lumped into a "minority" category, which denied individual ethnic identity, when using the federal guidelines. However, if the Washington State guideline was used in a multiracial setting, a school without a single white student could still not be segregated if it contained, for instance, thirty-nine percent black, thirty-nine percent Asian American, eleven percent Hispanic, and eleven percent Native American students. It seemed that it would be difficult to defend the Washington State definition in court as it applied to multiracial Seattle.

Other definitions of racial imbalance also existed in the community. One had been developed by the Church Council in its December 14, 1976, "statement on pluralism." The Council suggested a dual definition, one applying to schools which were predominately black and one applying to schools which had both a black and an Asian American population. The Church Council definition stated that students should be housed in schools on the basis of numerical equality, thereby defining some schools as having fifty percent black/fifty percent white student bodies (with the black population given a sixty percent ceiling), and others as having a one-third black, one-third Asian American and one-third white population (with a forty percent ceiling for either the black or the Asian population).

The Seattle Urban League had a definition of segregation in its Triad Plan, written in 1964 (plus-or-minus fifty percent of the average minority population.)[38] The NAACP has a national guideline of full integration: equal racial percentages in all schools. The League of Women Voters suggested a definition similar to the one developed by the Church Council and DWAC.[39]

DWAC adopted a definition of racial imbalance on the Monday before the June 8 School Board meeting, at the urging of representatives of the Church Council and School Board members. The DWAC definition was a dual one. In triracial schools (southeast Seattle) the combined minority population would not exceed seventy percent, with no more than forty percent of a single minority. In single ethnic minority schools (the central area), the minority percentage would not exceed twenty percent plus the districtwide minority average.

School district legal counsel Gary Little suggested that the Board adopt the definition of twenty percent above the districtwide average, plus fifty percent of a single minority as a more legally defensible definition.

The debate over the definition of racial imbalance during the School Board meeting of June 8 was lengthy and included two breaks during which Board members discussed the question with members of the community.[40]

Looking back on the decision, Board members are glad that they adopted the definition they did rather than a less stringent one. As Cheryl Bleakney says, "I'm not sorry about what we did adopt. In retrospect I'm glad it wasn't any higher [the permitted minority group percentages]."[41] The percentage of racial minority group students in the district has continued to increase yearly (as it had previously), raising the permitted total minority percentage to sixty percent (twenty percent above the combined districtwide minority percentage of forty percent) for the 1980–81 school year.

Seattle's dual definition of racial imbalance recognizes the uniqueness of the city, which unlike most cities experiencing public school desegregation, was desegregating a multiracial, not a biracial, population, and recognizing the individual characteristics of the city, where the central area schools were predominately black and southeast area schools were multiracial. By desegregating schools through its own action, Seattle was able to tailor a number of aspects of the Seattle Plan, including the definition of segregation. Input from the community on the definition was also apparent. While the need for a dual definition probably was self-evident because of the nature of the racial composition of the schools, the form of the definition was, at least in part, the result of the active voice of the Asian community, insisting that they not be grouped with others into one "minority" category, and the work of such groups as the Church Council of Greater Seattle and DWAC.

A fair amount of community input was solicited on other aspects of the June 8 resolutions before they were adopted. Shan Mullin of the Municipal League read them and commented to the superintendent. Probably representatives of city government and DWAC did so as well. The resolutions were given to representatives of the ACLU, the NAACP and the Church Council, for review and comment, on the Friday before the June 8 vote. The ACLU was scheduled to vote at its board meeting, Saturday, June 4, to sue the school district. ACLU made some small changes in the resolutions and agreed not to sue as long as the Board continued along the path outlined in the resolutions. The possible plaintiff groups were ecstatic at the content of the resolutions. A lawsuit was avoided.

Most of Seattle's population in general seemed not to understand the significance of the School Board's action on June 8. Though the Board meeting was well covered by the press, little criticism of the Board's action came from the public. One reason for this apparent apathy may have been that the public had heard the School Board decide to desegregate before, and then not take any definite action to do so. As Patt Sutton recalls,

Dr. Moberly kept saying, "Why aren't we hearing from people?" Cheryl and I told him, "Just wait. We'll hear from them." Dr. Moberly kept saying, "I can't believe this." We kept saying, "It's okay." We'd done things before. People had gotten all upset and then nothing had happened. Later, when people were howling at the doors, we said, "See!"[42]

It was probably not until November of 1977 that the general public understood that this time the School Board meant business.

Having told the superintendent what the ultimate goal was to be, the School Board then began to narrow the almost limitless number of options for a potential Seattle Plan, by adopting criteria for the plan.

CHAPTER 10

EQUALIZATION OF STUDENT TRANSFERS, AND ETHNIC IDENTITY

In February 1977 the District-Wide Advisory Committee on Desegregation developed thirteen criteria to use to evaluate desegregation plans. In April, Cheryl Bleakney met with Chairperson Dick Andrews and other individuals from DWAC to discuss those criteria. In May the School Board adopted eighteen criteria similar to DWAC's. In July, when DWAC asked the Board to identify "threshold criteria" — those criteria which were the most important — the School Board identified two, stating that it:

- Would place no greater burden on minority than majority students.
- Recognizes the need for ethnic identity of different minority students, and is sensitive to ethnic heritage (strong feeling that small minority groups should not be divided and scattered — that we should encourage transfer of minority students in large enough groups to maintain a sense of cohesiveness).[1]

As Bleakney recalls:

In early spring, Dick Andrews had brought us some criteria that DWAC had adopted. That looked to me like a good way for us [the Board] to take some initiative with the administration. I talked with Dick about the fact that I thought it would be really good if the Board adopted criteria. He said he thought so, too. And I said, "Well, I don't like the ones that DWAC adopted." So I set up a Saturday meeting with Dick and members of DWAC. I brought in some criteria which I liked better. We kicked them around and refined them. Then I went to Moberly and Don Olson and said, "I think it's really important that we adopt criteria." And they looked at me as though they thought I was crazy. At this point it was criteria to examine contingency plans [a backup to the Magnet Plan]. The criteria were actually adopted on May 11.[2]

Then in the summer, as we were going into a full-fledged development of a plan, DWAC again came to us and said, "Are there any threshold criteria that must be satisfied?" We pulled out two. The Board unanimously accepted them.[3]

After the community's review of the five planning models for a Seattle Plan, additional criteria emerged, including predictability, stability, consistent feeder patterns and keeping neighborhoods of students together. The importance of these criteria became clear in discussions of alternate desegregation strategies in the community during the fall of 1977.

Though there were some differences between DWAC's criteria and the School Board's, they were not substantially different. Using its criteria, DWAC concluded that a "fixed-assignment with options" plan was the best for Seattle. The School Board reached the same conclusion using its criteria.

With criteria established, actual planning could proceed. William Maynard's approach to desegregation planning began with the development of a continuum which indicated the amount of choice available to parents and students in various approaches to desegregation. The ends of the continuum were mandatory random reassignment (which provided the least choice) and open enrollment (which provided the most choice). (See chart 2.) The continuum served as a vehicle for discussing the controversial subject of "voluntary" versus "mandatory" desegregation, by pointing out that neither term describes a pure approach to desegregation. Rather, various desegregation strategies which could be used in Seattle could be described as more or less "voluntary" or more or less "mandatory." Before the Seattle Plan was adopted, students in Seattle were required to attend their neighborhood schools (fifth strategy from the bottom), unless they participated in the voluntary racial transfer program (second strategy from the bottom) or were reassigned for middle school desegregation (extreme top of continuum).

The Magnet Plan initiated during the 1977–78 school year was the most voluntary of the strategies on the continuum (Magnet Add-On Programs). The final Seattle Plan actually employs a number of the strategies outlined on Maynard's continuum (modified feeder patterns, grade reconfiguration, clustering and zoning, and school pairings). In addition, the voluntary racial transfer program continued in operation, and some schools continued to operate as total school magnets or contained magnet add-on programs but were not a part of grade-reconfigured pairs. Some programs were also relocated to assist with desegregation.

While the continuum was used by the desegregation planning office and

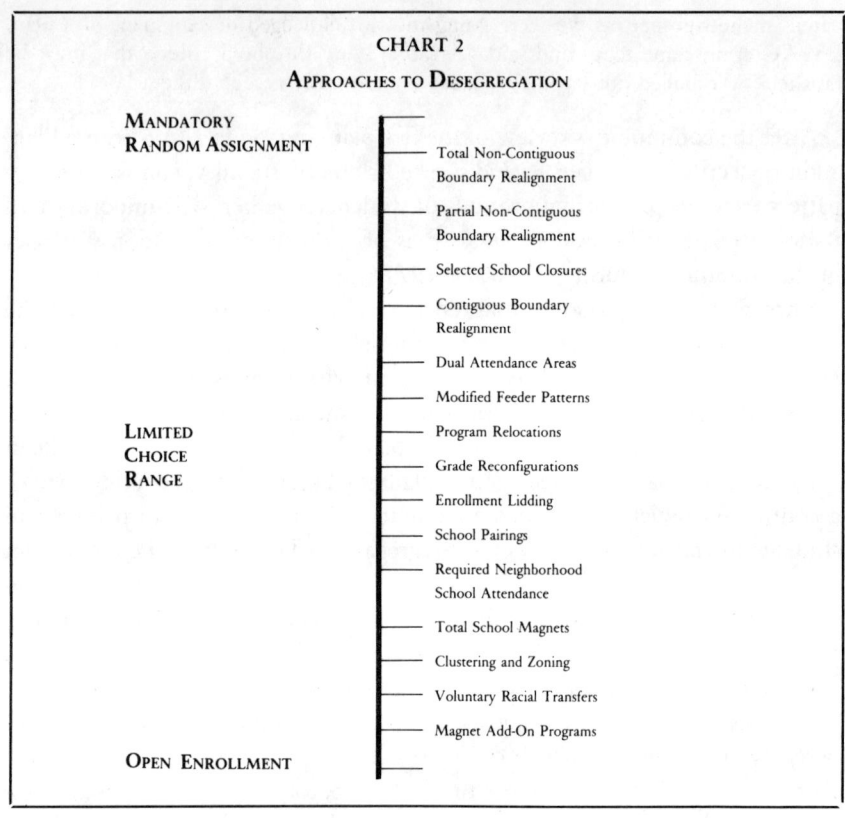

SOURCE: Dr. William Maynard, "The Seattle Plan: An Educationally Sound Approach to Desegregation/Integration," unpublished paper (no date), p. 2.

discussed in the community, Maynard never was given an opportunity to present his continuum to the School Board for their discussion.

In a paper entitled, "The Seattle Plan: An Educationally Sound Approach to Desegregation/Integration," Maynard outlined his philosophy of desegregation. The approach emphasizes two concepts: "quality education" and "integration for all children." According to Maynard, the following components are critical to an educationally sound desegregation strategy:

1. Equal educational opportunities;
2. Provisions for safety;
3. Educational options (including various teaching strategies to

complement student learning styles, curricula content, and programs to meet the special needs of students);

4. A curriculum which includes an emphasis on basic skills, multiethnic/multicultural education, career readiness education and sex equality education;

5. Provisions for the maintenance of ethnic identity for both majority and minority students;

6. High academic achievement expectations for each student;

7. Assurance that every child can succeed in school.

This was the goal of the Seattle Plan for Maynard.

By the time the School Board had adopted its enabling resolution on June 8, 1977, considerable direct communication, which contributed to the outcome of the Board's decision, was going on between some of the community's leaders and several of the members of the Board and school administration. Several structured communication forums existed which are discussed in other chapters – DWAC, the No-Name Committee (see Chapter 11), and the People Power Forums, the latter taking place primarily before the June 8 resolutions.

Though the general public did not seem to take the School Board's action seriously until November, leaders in numerous community organizations were well informed about what was happening. In addition the press covered activities well, and several radio stations did special programming. KING Radio ran public service announcements several times a day from January through December 1977, pointing out the key issues being debated. KING-TV also ran special public service announcements. A series of special press conferences were coordinated by People Power, as well as special briefings for the staffs of KING and KOMO television.

Education committees in the Chamber of Commerce, the Municipal League, the League of Women Voters, the Church Council of Greater Seattle, the American Friends Service Committee, the Japanese American Citizens' League, the Seattle Urban League, the Seattle chapter of the NAACP, the ACLU of Washington, the Central Area School Council, the Committee for Southeast Seattle Schools, the Asian American Education Association, the Seattle Teachers Association, Seattle Council PTSA, the Coalition for Quality Integrated Education, and many more groups were discussing the issues. City government was involved through the Office of

Policy Planning. Communication between these groups took place at DWAC and through the No-Name Committee. Despite all of this, it is safe to say that probably only a small percentage of the population of the city really knew what was happening.[4] However, because community leaders were so well informed and had been involved in the School Board's decision, when opposition to desegregation did surface, it gained no support from any previously organized group in Seattle.

This high level of discussion on an issue under consideration by the Seattle School Board was unusual. Community groups have never before or since become so actively involved in a public school issue. At the same time individuals strongly opposed to mandatory forms of desegregation were extremely quiet, despite efforts by Board member Ellen Roe to encourage their participation.

Seattle was about to embark on its second "mandatory" desegregation effort. Moberly had discussed the first mandatory plan, the middle school desegregation effort, with other people in Seattle and had developed an opinion about that first plan which influenced his approach to desegregation planning in 1977. According to Moberly:

The Middle School Plan was mandatory, but it really wasn't a mandatory plan. It was tied to a controversial educational philosophy. It was mandatory, but there were many ways of getting out of it. A comprehensive desegregation plan at that time would have been a much more viable thing.

I was not here, so I do not have the advantage of having lived through it firsthand. I've talked to people and had a lot of reactions on both sides. At that time you were mixing desegregation and an educational philosophy — both were radical changes. You could say you disliked the plan on educational grounds and still be nice. You didn't have to be racist to be against the Middle School Plan. I think mixing desegregation and an educational philosophy is bad.[5] I don't think that is the way to get anything done. If your goal is desegregation, go out and desegregate and don't throw in a controversial educational philosophy.

That plan was developed, partially because of no open-meeting law, behind closed doors, and a gigantic volume was thrown out to the public and they didn't understand it.

Also I think things were changed socially in this country between 1971 and 1977. There were some strides made in this country. Some people changed their viewpoints. I think the energy of the CAMB [Citizens Against Mandatory Busing] group has dissipated. They fought and lost.

I did not want to become a bleeding-heart liberal, standing out there. I could not have come into this town to save Seattle on a white horse charging down on the desegregation issue. If desegregation focused on one person you could have had an aborted plan with me losing my job.

My personal commitment is to do a good job, a professional job. I have a high level of professional integrity in doing my job well.

I work for a majority of the School Board. I do not have the right to make independent decisions for the city.[6]

Proposed desegregation planning alternatives were scheduled to be completed by October. On September 9, five possible models were presented verbally to DWAC. The Seattle Urban League had also dusted off its 1964 Triad Plan and rewritten it with current data, and was submitting it for consideration. The Board had indicated that anyone could submit a plan for consideration. Five plans, four written by the district plus the Urban League's Triad Plan, were published in late September under the title, *Proposed Alternative Desegregation Plans: Options for Eliminating Imbalance by the 1979-80 School Year: The Seattle Plan.* The document included a preface with historical information, maps, a glossary of terms and a section entitled, "Basic Desegregation Services Provided to Any Plan to Eliminate Racial Imbalance by the 1979-80 School Year." The total document was 425 pages long. A summary was also prepared. One of the plans written by the district (Plan II) was a boundary realignment plan based on the Denver, Colorado, plan. Elementary attendance boundaries were redrawn to include "islands" from other attendance areas to achieve racial balance. That plan was purely mandatory, based on new student school assignments. Plans I, III and IV were modified magnet school plans which employed a voluntary student recruitment effort each year to magnet schools and a mandatory reassignment backup if insufficient numbers of students transferred voluntarily. Of these, Plan IV included some additional elements such as "zoning," which restricted the opportunities for voluntary transfers to cut down on transportation costs. The fifth plan, the Urban League's Triad Plan, based on the model of a "Princeton Plan," created clusters of three elementary schools, changing the grade configuration of those schools in order that students from all three elementary attendance areas could attend one of three schools for grades one and two, a second school for grades three and four, and the third for grades five and six. Secondary feeder patterns[7] were then readjusted to desegregate those schools.

It was not necessarily assumed that Seattle would select one of these plans. All would be reviewed, and the final plan might include elements of more than one of the plans.

The five planning models were reviewed by community organizations, analyzed in detail by DWAC, and presented to the public at thirty meetings held throughout the city between October 13 and November 15. Community reaction to the plans was tabulated through a questionnaire.

The School Board discussed a number of issues during the fall of 1977 that would have impact on the plan. Facilities was one of the issues. Most of the schools which contained large numbers of black and Asian students were overenrolled, while schools in predominately white areas of Seattle were underutilized. It was apparent that at some point Seattle, like most school districts, would have to consider closing schools.[8] The size of a building also determined the number of students it could house. During October the Board adopted a standard to define the capacity of a building and made other facilities-related decisions, including one which determined that if a school was closed, students in that building would be treated no differently from other students in the desegregation plan. This decision meant that Seattle would not desegregate schools by closing minority impacted schools and sending those students out to predominately white schools. Instead students would be assigned to schools adjacent to the ones closed. Two schools were closed that year — Fairview, a white school, and Hawthorne, a multiracial school, closed for earthquake safety reasons. Hawthorne students were not assigned to adjacent schools despite School Board policy, but now attend school away from their neighborhood at the school with which the Hawthorne community was paired.[9]

CHAPTER 11

IT HELPS TO TALK ABOUT IT

After the School Board had decided to eliminate segregation on June 8, a lawsuit was not needed. However, the threat of a possible suit continued in the event the Board did not follow through with its June 8 commitment.

Legal Pressure Still Present

On Saturday, June 4, four days before the School Board adopted its enabling resolutions defining racial imbalance and setting a timetable to eliminate it, the board of directors of the ACLU of Washington directed legal counsel to immediately prepare for filing in U.S. District Court litigation alleging that the Seattle schools were maintaining a segregated system in violation of the Fourteenth Amendment to the U.S. Constitution, and "further directs counsel to commence such litigation if and when the board of directors of Seattle School District #1 refuses to pursue or fails to accomplish"[1] any of the actions outlined in the proposed School Board resolutions (1977-8 and 1977-9). The ACLU resolution further directed ACLU staff, desegregation task force and legal counsel to maintain communication with the signers of the May 20 letter — the other organizations committed to sue the school district — and with the school district itself.

In addition, the Task Force on Racial Justice of the Church Council was following through with its procedure for gaining approval of the board of directors of the Church Council to be a party in a suit.

At the first meeting of the executive committee of the Church Council's board (the last Friday in May) following the task force decision to recommend suing, the resolution authorizing a suit was presented by members of the task force. The Executive Committee approved the resolution, recommending its passage to the Board with two provisions. First, an amendment was added to the resolution indicating that the suit would not be filed until sufficient funds had been secured to begin, and second, the Executive Committee asked that the task force call a meeting to discuss the possible legal action with representatives of the churches in the greater Seattle area.

A letter dated May 31 was sent to each church in the greater Seattle area and to individuals who had participated in the council's education program on desegregation, inviting everyone to a meeting on June 7 at St. Mark's Episcopal Cathedral for the purposes of discussing the possibility of the Church Council's becoming a plaintiff in the suit. All members of the Church Council board of directors were invited, though the meeting was not intended as an action meeting. A panel presentation was made, including information on the role of the plaintiffs, strategies for joint legal action, a review of the Church Council's position statement and recommendations from the task force regarding the lawsuit. About sixty individuals attended the meeting, listened to the panel (ACLU lawyer Fred Noland; Gary Higashi, president of the Asian American Education Association — which was also considering joining in the suit; Tom Lemley, Church Council legal counsel; and Ann Siqueland), and asked questions. An anonymous questionnaire was also distributed to poll opinions on the actions considered by the council. Of the twenty-five questionnaires returned, only one indicated disagreement with the recommendation to join the lawsuit. When the board of directors of the Church Council voted on the recommendation on June 14, 1977, the vote authorizing the council to sue the School Board was unanimous.

Obviously every individual sitting in every church pew in the greater Seattle area did not agree that the Church Council should take legal action against the School Board to end segregation, but the council had done its homework well enough — by keeping churches and church leaders informed of its actions and developments in the city on the subject of desegregation — that the council took this serious step with a substantial part of its constituency behind it.

Funds were secured to make the suit possible,[2] and a third-year law student from the University of Washington, Gary Iwamoto, was hired in the fall of 1977 to continue the legal research begun by the ACLU and the NAACP for a possible lawsuit. Iwamoto worked until December 14, when the School Board adopted the Seattle Plan. He was supervised by both the Church Council and by Fred Noland, who it was agreed would be head legal counsel in any joint action against the School Board. Iwamoto's handwritten complaint, prepared under Noland's direction, charging the Seattle School Board with intentional segregation, is still on file in the Church Council's office. It was never typed.

The matter of a lawsuit was a serious one, but William Cate of the Church Council never indicated any hesitancy to sue, should that be necessary:

We can build on that litigation. The next time we decide to enter into a legal situation, people will not be so surprised. This opened the door and we were successful. I must confess, I was as afraid as anyone because I never had been involved in a lawsuit. I think you grow in those kinds of experiences; you grow in your approaches to strategizing on how you can effect community change; we learned a great deal in desegregation about how you do that. The beauty of it is that in a place like Seattle, the voluntary sector could put itself together well enough to move the School Board. I have a feeling that Dr. Moberly never knew quite what happened in terms of the community dynamics.[3]

One member of the Task Force on Racial Justice in Education, David Colwell, had misgivings when the task force decided to recommend suing. Later, he recalls the reasons for his hesitation:

At that time I was trying to keep everybody somewhat in step. What I was doing was sort of slowing down the process to make sure we were going through the process and would not make a premature, too rapid, decision in that regard. But I have no problem with justification of the suit, because when you've got a situation where persons of presumed good will cannot agree, the American way of doing things is to take it to court. I was anxious at that time not to cause alienation between the Chamber of Commerce and Municipal League and those of us involved in the suit. And there was a very real danger of that. It didn't happen, and I'm grateful it didn't happen, and I think in retrospect that the suit is a vital ingredient in the whole process. There may have been temporary alienation.[4]

As a member of the board of the Municipal League, Colwell was in communication with Shan Mullin, president of the league, who was working to forestall a suit until the School Board could be persuaded to take action on its own.

During the time that the Seattle Plan was being developed, the pressure of a possible lawsuit was maintained by the expanded plaintiff group. While the district was taking definitive action to end segregation, there was no point in filing a suit, and even if one had been filed, the likelihood of receiving an early court date was minimal. However, joint plaintiffs continued to watch, and

Gary Iwamoto continued to plow through School Board files and review the evidence already gathered by the NAACP and the ACLU. This was a conscious effort to keep pressure on the school district to keep their June 8 promise.

Communication Networks: What's In a Name?

One particular communications effort was initiated, in part, to keep communications lines open with those who had considered suing the district. Shan Mullin called it the Desegregation Coordination Group, and he should know because Mullin is primarily responsible for its existence and is the person who served until March 1978 as the group's "temporary interim convenor."[5] Almost everyone else called it the "No-Name" Committee or the noncommittee. The group was one of the most viable communication links which existed between community organizations beginning in mid-June 1977 and lasting through the implementation of the Seattle Plan. The purpose of the committee was to prevent potential adversaries from misunderstanding each other. It was also one of the places where many issues surrounding the development of the Seattle Plan were discussed. The group was a relatively closed one, and no one from the press was ever present.

The superintendent had wanted a blue-ribbon committee of two hundred people to serve as a public relations group, advocating desegregation to the larger community. He had proposed this idea at a meeting held at the Washington Athletic Club on Monday, June 6. Richard Andrews, David Colwell (chair of the Church Council Task Force), and Board members Don Olson and Patt Sutton were present, along with Shan Mullin and Katherine Bullitt from the Municipal League, Walt Williams and Russ Amick from the Chamber of Commerce, and Olaf Kvamme, Seattle schools' intergovernmental relations staff person. The superintendent did not get much support for his idea.

According to Richard Andrews, David Colwell had the most impact upon preventing the establishment of the blue-ribbon committee. Colwell told the superintendent that he did not have much confidence that the district would follow through on the School Board's proposed June 8 resolutions, and he would not be an advocate for the district until he was sure there was something to advocate for.[6]

The discussion at the meeting convinced Shan Mullin that something else was needed. He recalls:

The whole thing [The No-Name Committee] came out of a conversation with Moberly and others about having a blue-ribbon committee in addition to DWAC. I said, "I don't think that [the blue-ribbon committee] is going to work. You're asking for a committee before you have anything concrete to show them. Your big problem now is the different points of view held by your active groups. Somehow they need to talk with each other. If they don't they are going to go off in different directions. You've got to build trust by some means of regular dialogue."[7]

That is what the No-Name Committee did.

Mullin invited individuals who were active in the organizations which were threatening to sue the school district (NAACP, ACLU, Church Council and AAEA), the signers of the May 20 joint letter (the city, Seattle Urban League, Municipal League and Chamber of Commerce) and DWAC. Members of the League of Women Voters, the Seattle Council PTSA, the Coalition for Quality Integrated Education and the People Power Coalition were also invited to participate. The groups represented included the active organizations represented on DWAC, with one significant exception. The ACLU had chosen not to participate on DWAC after threatening to sue the school district, but they actively participated on the No-Name Committee.

Organizations were often represented on the No-Name Committee by different individuals from those serving on DWAC. School Board members were occasionally invited to meetings, and Olaf Kvame from the district was usually present.

The No-Name Committee first met on June 27 in the conference room at Mullin's law office. The agenda Mullin prepared for the meeting pointed out the need to look at the total picture of desegregation and to look at desegregation from a positive point of view, keeping educational objectives in mind.

The group met periodically when there was an issue which needed discussion. No one on the No-Name Committee was considered an official representative from his or her organization. Individuals talked from their own point of view and exchanged information about what their organizations were doing. In some cases consensus was developed around an approach to a particular problem. At one meeting the role the School Board would play in making the final decision on a plan was discussed. School Board members attending that meeting realized that the final process had not been well defined and proceeded to remedy the situation.

ACLU members David Harrison, Dan Levant and Fred Noland found the

No-Name Committee to be very effective. It was their primary communication link with other groups working on desegregation. Richard Andrews appreciated the group because the press was not present and meetings gave him an opportunity to discuss the problems he was having as chair of DWAC.

For those who were not members of DWAC, but who were decision-makers in their respective organizations (e.g., Jerome Page, the Urban League; David Colwell, the Church Council; Shelly Yapp, the city's Office of Policy Planning; Shan Mullin and Eben Carlson, the Municipal League; and Russ Amick, the Chamber of Commerce), the No-Name Committee provided an opportunity to discuss issues face-to-face and remain informed on what other groups were doing.

When the No-Name Committee began to meet, there was little trust between individuals from groups threatening to sue the school district on one side, and the Municipal League and the Chamber of Commerce on the other. Because each individual present discussed his/her own point of view directly instead of having that position communicated by stories in the press or through second- or third-hand reports, there was little chance that misunderstanding would take place. Everyone did not agree, but everyone knew the position taken by the major active groups involved in the desegregation effort. Seattle thereby avoided a schism between individuals and groups on opposing sides of the discussion concerning strategies for desegregating schools. Or, at least, disagreements did not get blown out of proportion through rumor or extensive press coverage. While openness in a democratic decision-making process is definitely desirable, with an issue as potentially emotional as desegregation, attention is best paid to keeping lines of communication open.

The No-Name Committee has been described as "elitist."

The politics of school desegregation, then, was "managed" by a group of community elites who, through their respective and influential organizations, formed a close network in order to communicate, bargain, and compromise with one another. If the Seattle Plan was defined in any one place it was here. . . . All [of the members of the No-Name Committee] were solidly middle-class and professional. Lawyers, businessmen, civic leaders and university professors represented the core of the group.[8]

In fact, the politics of desegregation in Seattle were far more complicated.

Though the communications role the No-Name Committee played is significant, it is not accurate to suggest that the Seattle Plan was defined by the

No-Name Committee. Most of the decisions which contributed to the adoption of the Seattle Plan had already been made before the No-Name Committee began meeting. The definition of racial imbalance was set; the timetable to desegregate was established; the criteria which would determine the plan were established; the framework of the plan that would ultimately be adopted, the Urban League's Triad Plan, was in existence; and the dynamics which kept the process in motion, including an impending lawsuit and pressure from city government, were well in place. The No-Name Committee did see itself as central to the process for establishing a desegregation plan for Seattle, but the deciding recommendation on the nature of the Seattle Plan – the major decision left to be made after the No-Name Committee was formed – was made by DWAC by passing a motion made by an individual who did not attend any No-Name Committee meetings prior to making her motion. DWAC, rather than the No-Name Committee, was the advisory body for community input during the process for developing the Seattle Plan. And that is appropriate, as it was the official avenue for community involvement, duly constituted by the district, covered by the press and open to the public.

Communications Network: DWAC

From June 1977 to December 1977 desegregation was discussed, not in terms of whether or not the city was going to end public school segregation, but in terms of *how* it was going to end public school segregation. Richard Andrews consistently said that Seattle would do it in "a just, right and equitable" manner.

While the school administration was developing planning models between June and September of 1977 for community review, DWAC was analyzing student transfer strategies to accomplish desegregation. The committee identified every possible "displacement strategy" and every possible "replacement strategy"; that is, ways to move students out of school buildings and ways to move them into new buildings. Each strategy that the committee could think of or find in already existing desegregation plans across the country was analyzed by listing all of its advantages and disadvantages and comparing it to DWAC's criteria. This time-consuming exercise helped DWAC to better focus the issues which were important to it. When the five planning models were released by the district (including the one written by the Seattle Urban League), DWAC broke up into committees and analyzed each model according to their thirteen criteria and their analysis of student transfer strategies. DWAC members also conducted the thirty community hearings which invited input from the general public on the five planning models. In addition some DWAC members were participating in other types of community education on desegregation. Arlene Oki spent a considerable amount of time keeping various Asian organizations informed, and trying to recruit more Asian representation on DWAC. Arlis Stewart worked with the media to encourage coverage of the issues under discussion. The Church Council was conducting adult-education classes in area churches. Numerous discussions were taking place in black community organizations.

Along with DWAC, most community organizations were involved in their own assessment of the planning models under review between September and November. Many specifically reviewed the Urban League's Triad Plan.

Communications Network: Black and Asian Communities

The Seattle Urban League had begun to rewrite its 1964 Triad Plan with current student enrollment data in April 1977. Cheryl Crawford, Urban League education director, had the responsibility for the rewrite. The league hired Ivan King as a consultant to assist with the project; King had worked for the Urban League in 1964 and had done a substantial amount of the work on the first Triad Plan. Arlis Stewart also offered to assist.

By June, the Triad Plan had been rewritten, but when the district reviewed it, district planners felt that the plan would not be compatible with other plans the district would be writing because the student data base used by the Urban League was not the same as the data base the district would be using. (The district planned to use data based on where students lived in the district; the Urban League had used information concerning student enrollment in schools. Many students attended schools outside the attendance area in which they resided.) With some assistance from the district, the Triad Plan was again rewritten to reflect resident data in order to be included with the four plans written by district planners.

Beginning on June 10 a series of meetings was called by the Urban League to explain the Triad Plan to leaders of various organizations. The June 10 meeting included representatives from most of the organizations with membership on DWAC. Later, presentations were made to individual organizations on request.

Cheryl Crawford had become acutely aware of the possible conflict between members of the Asian and black communities during the June 8

School Board meeting; she had witnessed an argument between Dorothy Hollingsworth and Arlene Oki over the definition of racial imbalance. The Urban League, therefore, was especially concerned about the Asian community's feelings on the Triad Plan, and particular attention was paid to soliciting opinions from members of the Asian community. Gary Higashi remembers this period:

The Urban League invited Asians to review the Triad Plan. It was a very astute thing to do. There is a general attitude among blacks that Asians are not minority people, Japanese in particular. They believe that the Japanese have taken advantage of the system and are a part of the problem. You don't see this as much in this city as elsewhere. And there is a reluctance on the part of the Asian community to identify with blacks. So it was a good move on Jerome Page's part to talk about the Triad Plan with Asians. He was very careful not to single out just black children in his conversations. That attitude, along with the meetings which were held, were a tremendous effort at creating good relations between Asians and blacks, and it speaks well for the Urban League.

I remember feeling at the meeting [June 10] that we had been invited to take part and have a say in what the Urban League was going to propose to the school district. They listened to us very carefully. It was not just a cursory thing. We made some recommendations including one on bilingual education.[9]

The Urban League's conscientious effort to solicit ideas for the Triad Plan helped greatly in insuring that Asians would support the Triad Plan as a model for the Seattle Plan. Generally, they did.

In addition, a series of meetings between blacks and Asians, sometimes referred to as "black and yellow meetings," were held following the June 8 Board resolutions. These meetings, by and large, were organized by Jerome Page, with the intention of ironing out any differences which might still exist between Asians and blacks. The conversations were successful, and were an important part of Seattle's ability to desegregate schools with such a broad base of community support.

CHAPTER 12

WHICH COMES FIRST?

When the time came to decide on the final plan to desegregate Seattle Public Schools, a controversy developed between individuals who wanted to desegregate by first allowing students to voluntarily change schools (with a mandatory reassignment backup) and those who wanted to "fix the assignment" of students first, to assure racial balance.

William Maynard, head of the desegregation office, remembers the decision on the final plan:

The structure of the final plan really evolved over a period of time, and Dick Andrews is probably the key person that influenced me. Those seven elements in that final plan that I shared with the superintendent evolved from Dick and me. I think Dick convinced me that the voluntary first plan with a mandatory backup wouldn't work.

One of the biggest problems was that my lead planners were misinterpreting information, giving misinterpretations of information to show that it [a fixed-assignment plan] would never work. In fact, they wouldn't even write the final plan.

But in discussions with Dick Andrews and Dick Dyksterhuis, I began to see how to do it. I didn't share that information with the superintendent for a long time, probably three or four weeks, until I was actually certain.

I couldn't give out information on the direction we were moving [to the DWAC Core Committee] because if it got out, I'd have been blown away.

I was having an internal battle[1]

Maynard's comments describe the climate in the school district in late October and early November of 1977 when the decision to write a final plan was being made. The planners did not agree on a plan for Seattle, and they had not been given any direction.

Knowing of the internal controversy in the planning staff, Superintendent

Moberly reviewed the five planning models under consideration Friday evening, November 5:

When it got right down to be finalized, I looked at the options I had. I spent one weekend getting ready for the staff to give them their final directions. I spent some time at home with the five plans. I gave the staff the planning directions Saturday morning [November 6, 1977].

I could not support a voluntary version with a mandatory backup because it meant instability every year. It meant aggressive recruitment of students on the part of the administration every year.

I gave clear directions as to what I wanted the final product to be and that was the fixed-assignment plan.[2]

The superintendent's copy of his instructions to the staff are hand-written on a yellow legal-size tablet page. The points include:

- A heavy emphasis on academic achievement and advanced placement;
- A phase-in of the high schools and junior highs and middle schools;
- To maintain the voluntary racial transfer program and the magnets;
- To set up a zone situation to minimize the busing;
- To build in continuity of feeder patterns, K-12;
- Preserve present integrated schools and build in lids for the future;
- Go with pairs and triads, with the mandatory assignment, and build in those local options.

Board member Cheryl Bleakney remembers the first part of November:

There was a breakdown in the staff, a complete breakdown. Everytime the desegregation planners would start down one way [to write a final plan], there developed a division between the planners.

I got a call in the middle of November [twelfth or thirteenth]. The planners were locked up someplace. Things had absolutely broken down. They were doing absolutely the wrong thing — totally wrong.

So we scheduled a meeting the next morning in Bill Maynard's office. That's when we clarified why the planners were having so much trouble. They felt they couldn't guarantee a desegregation plan with paired schools if you had options in it.[3] And we said you could if you controlled where the options went.

At that point Dick Andrews and I went down to see the superintendent and told him he had an insurrection among his troops and he had to do something about it. I told him quite frankly that he didn't dare have a plan that didn't have the support of

DWAC and Suzanne, Dorothy and I. I think Dorothy put a lot of pressure on him, too.[4]

The questionnaires filled out at the thirty community meetings held in Seattle on the five planning models favored one of the voluntary-first planning models written by the district, at least in the predominately white areas of town. However, these same people also wanted students in individual neighborhoods kept together, impossible in a voluntary plan.[5] Parents in minority impacted areas of Seattle, the central and southeast areas, tended to favor the "fixed-assignment" Triad Plan.

The parents of children who were participating in the Magnet School Plan that year organized themselves to support the voluntary-first approach to desegregation, fearing that a mandatory, fixed-assignment triad-type plan would deprive them of the specialized programs their children were enjoying. This was predominately a white group of parents, as recruitment to magnets had focused on moving white students. Of the total number of questionnaires (1,002) compiled by the district on the community's preference on desegregation planning models, 259 came from a meeting of magnet parents, virtually all favoring one of the voluntary-first approaches. The final tabulation of the 1,002 questionnaires showed the order of preference as Plan III, Plan I (voluntary plans with a mandatory backup), and the Triad Plan. It is likely that many people favoring the voluntary-first plans opposed all forms of mandatory desegregation and may not even have entirely realized that mandatory assignment would take place under Plans I and III.

Both the School Board's threshold criteria and DWAC's criteria emphasized equal student transfers between predominately white communities and communities which were predominately black or multiracial, and keeping students together in large enough ethnic groups to maintain ethnic identity. These goals were more easily reached with a paired school approach (the mandatory fixed-assignment triad model),[6] because for every building attended in large numbers by black and Asian students, there was at least one building of white students to be reassigned. Because most white impacted schools were smaller than most schools defined as racially imbalanced, in some cases two white schools were paired (technically, a "split pair" but sometimes called a triad) with the segregated school. This approach also kept neighborhood groups of students together.

During October, community groups had begun to state their preference for the final Seattle Plan. The League of Women Voters indicated a preference for mandatory desegregation. The Church Council Task Force on Racial Justice in Education made the front page of the *Seattle Times* on Saturday, October 22, as the result of the decision it had made on that day, favoring the "fixed-assignment-first approach" — the first group to publicly state that preference. Dick Andrews and Board members Cheryl Bleakney and Suzanne Hittman recall discussing in mid-October what they wanted to see in a fixed-assignment plan with options. Bleakney shared a written outline of her ideas with members of the administration and told the superintendent about it. Bill Maynard felt that he and Dick Andrews worked out the details of the plan in mid-October. Rob Makin of the Chamber of Commerce recalls that by mid-October most individuals actively involved on DWAC or the No-Name Committee could describe the final Seattle Plan.[7] A feeling of consensus was developing for a plan modeled on the Urban League's Triad Plan with some modifications. The superintendent says he decided what plan he would recommend on the evening of November 5. A coalition of black community groups called together by Jerome Page was developing its position through the middle of October, clearly favoring a mandatory fixed-assignment plan because it was the only approach which would produce any degree of equal student transfers. It was clear that most racial minority students would be changing schools and the minority communities wanted a guarantee that an equal number of white students would also be moving. Except for the Magnet Plan, all desegregation efforts in Seattle had moved more minority students than white: Specifically, almost eighty percent of the students who had moved for desegregation purposes in the voluntary racial transfer program, in operation since 1963, were black.

The debate over the final Seattle Plan was resolved by DWAC. In mid-October, Dick Andrews appointed a "Core Committee," composed of representatives from the Municipal League (Jerry Skutt), the Urban League (Cheryl Crawford), the NAACP (Connie Herring), the Asian community (Arlene Oki), and the Church Council (Ann Siqueland). Andrews felt that if he could get agreement from these individuals on a plan for Seattle, the plan would have a strong enough political base to survive. Connie Herring, Cheryl Crawford, Arlene Oki and Ann Siqueland probably had parallel ideas on desegregation. Jerry Skutt and the Municipal League were heading in a different direction. The Core Committee was to work with the school administration during the writing of the final plan. Because the group was appointed by Andrews rather than being elected by DWAC, and because of its potential power, Andrews received some criticism. DWAC members, however, knew that the Core Committee had been appointed and received reports on its progress. No member of DWAC objected to the committee's existence at any of the meetings of DWAC.

As the time approached when the final plan was to be written (mid-October), Jerry Skutt developed a list of questions to be used to identify the scope of that plan. Dick Andrews and Arlis Stewart helped write the questions, and DWAC was to discuss them while they were simultaneously being discussed by the Municipal League's and the Chamber of Commerce's education committees.

The Municipal League would have preferred that the school district adopt a plan with a voluntary student transfer phase and a mandatory backup. Jerry Skutt, who had well-developed planning skills, was attempting to develop a desegregation model employing the Municipal League point of view that would still satisfy the School Board's adopted guidelines. During the period when the district's administration was beginning to write the final plan, Skutt spent time working with the planners, discussing his ideas and those of the Municipal League. Skutt anticipated that the process of answering the questions he had developed would help lead DWAC, the Municipal League, the Chamber of Commerce and others to some consensus on the final plan for Seattle.

DWAC's Core Committee began to meet regularly with the administrative planners in mid-October to discuss the final Seattle Plan. Most Core Committee members expressed frustration about the meetings with district planners. With the exception of Jerry Skutt, the Core Committee members favored a fixed-assignment plan. Given the opportunity to have the plan the way they wanted it, they would have preferred program options to exist only within school buildings involved in pairs and triads, rather than that students be given the opportunity to transfer between school buildings to take advantage of program options.[8] On numerous occasions, members of the Core Committee explained their ideas to the district planners, who appeared to understand. However, at the next meeting between the planners and the Core Committee, the planners would describe the plan they were writing, and it would be a modified magnet school plan which relied on voluntary student transfers, with a mandatory backup. The Core Committee would again explain what they wanted the final plan to look like, again feel they had been understood, and again return to find the planners writing a voluntary-first magnet plan.

The conflict over what Seattle's final desegregation plan would look like came to a head on Wednesday evening, November 9. In an afternoon meeting between the Core Committee and the district planners, three members of the planning staff outlined for the Core Committee what the superintendent had directed them to do the previous Saturday. Each described an entirely different plan. Dick Dyksterhuis said that the superintendent had asked the planners to write a fixed-assignment plan with options, similar to the ideas of most Core Committee members. Bill Maynard, the director of the desegregation office, described a plan based on magnet schools, with five or six schools clustered together between which students could voluntarily move. A mandatory backup of an unspecified nature would be employed if voluntary efforts failed. The plan was consistent with Jerry Skutt's model. Bobby Hamilton, another planner, said that the superintendent had asked the planners to write a plan similar to the expanded magnet models (Plans I, III and IV) written by the district that fall for community review.[9] The meeting went on for several hours, with Core Committee members again attempting to describe the fixed-assignment plan they wanted to see. No one except Dick Dyksterhuis seemed to understand what they were saying.

In the middle of the meeting Dick Andrews received a call from his wife, Barbara. She had been sick and had taken her temperature, and it was 105 degrees. Andrews went home. The rest of the Core Committee stayed and began to discuss what they wanted in a desegregation plan, with the difference between Jerry Skutt's ideas and the rest of the committee's becoming quite apparent. It also had become increasingly apparent that the district had begun writing at least one plan. In order for a plan to be ready for the Board to adopt on December 14, if the School Board was going to meet its deadline, something had to be begun.[10] Community review of the five planning models would not be complete until November 15, and some Core Committee members felt that it was unfair for the final plan to be begun until community review was completed. Jerry Skutt was particularly concerned about this. However, it was clear that the planners were writing something, basically a voluntary student transfer magnet plan with a mandatory backup, and the superintendent had apparently given instructions on the kind of plan he wanted. If DWAC was going to have input into the final plan, most Core Committee members felt it had to happen soon.

142 Without a Court Order

An argument between Ann Siqueland and Jerry Skutt developed over the approach to desegregation. Skutt explained his ideas for the Seattle Plan, but did not specify how student transfers would occur in a mandatory backup, if voluntary efforts failed. Siqueland asked Skutt repeatedly how he was going to move the students if voluntary efforts failed, and did not feel she received an answer. Siqueland indicated that if Skutt made a motion that night at the DWAC meeting outlining his plan, she would not oppose him, being more concerned that DWAC recommend some plan rather than no plan. Skutt recalls that he and Siqueland disagreed over the timing of a DWAC recommendation. Skutt felt the process would be violated if a motion were made before the community review was over November 15.

Later, Dick Andrews returned. Barbara Andrews had taken her temperature with a broken thermometer, and she was not as sick as it appeared. Skutt turned to Andrews for support for his concerns, and Andrews said that if he had to choose between the ideas of members on the Core Committee on the subject of desegregation, as a white male he would have to side with the minority people and women in the group. The Core Committee broke up to have dinner before the 7:30 DWAC meeting. Jerry Skutt and Ann Siqueland went home to have dinner with their respective families. The rest of the Core Committee ate at a restaurant near the school district offices, the Brick Oven.

Several Asian community people showed up for the DWAC meeting who had not normally attended — two who were not members of DWAC. Most of DWAC's black members also arrived for the meeting. Knowing that the discussion of the final plan was going to take place that night, Arlis Stewart and Ann Siqueland had called minority community people, wanting them fully involved in the final DWAC decision on the plan. Cheryl Bleakney also arrived for the meeting, having been told by Arlis Stewart that the meeting would be an important one. Dick Andrews recalls that meeting:

At the previous DWAC meeting it had been announced that we would discuss a recommendation on the final plan.[11] I put the committee into a committee of the whole so that no motions were appropriate. DWAC discussed the matter of the final plan for hours. An individual on the committee, Ann Siqueland, said she wanted to make a motion, and I said that we were in the committee of the whole and as long as there was further discussion, unless the committee wanted to go out of the committee of the whole, we were not in a format to accept a motion. People started discussing again, and I said, "It's obvious that you are not ready to stop discussing." They continued discussing, and Ann said, "I still want to make my motion." And I said to the committee, "We are in the committee of the whole. I am willing to go out of the committee of the whole to accept this motion, but I'll only do it with the consent of the committee." Then another member of the committee said, "I'd like to hear the motion." And someone else said the same thing. And I said, "Unless I hear objections, I understood that you want to come out of the committee of the whole for the purpose of receiving a motion." Anybody at that time could have stopped that motion. Ann presented the motion verbally, and anyone there could have said, "I'm sorry. That's an important matter. I really want to see that motion in writing." No one did that. The committee discussed the motion for another hour, and then voted on it.[12]

The vote was eighteen-to-seven in favor of "a fixed-assignment-first plan with options" — the basis of the Seattle Plan. By the time the vote was taken, a few members of DWAC had gone home. There were a few abstentions on the motion, including Barbara Beuschlein's. She knew Jerry Skutt also had a motion, and she wanted to hear it before voting.[13] Nonmembers of DWAC in attendance did not vote.

Ann Siqueland decided to make the motion after the meeting was well under way because Jerry Skutt was making no effort to make the motion she had expected he would make. Siqueland also was convinced that a majority of DWAC favored a fixed-assignment plan. She represented the one community organization which had taken a public position favoring a fixed-assignment plan (with the exception of the Urban League, which would be expected to support the plan it had written).

Siqueland had not written out her motion but made it verbally. Cheryl Bleakney, sitting in the back of the room taking shorthand notes, as is her custom, had written the motion down. She offered to reread it just before the final vote was taken. Appearances to the contrary, Siqueland and Bleakney had never discussed a final outline for the Seattle Plan. Each, however, was aware of how the other felt about a desegregation plan for Seattle.

Dick Andrews says he was not certain the motion on a fixed-assignment plan would pass when it was made. In an attempt to persuade DWAC members to vote in favor of that motion, he stated his personal opinion, favoring a "fixed-assignment-first plan."

During the weeks prior to the DWAC motion, leaders of black community organizations had been meeting to develop a unified statement on the final Seattle Plan. While that statement had not been made public, it was abundantly clear that the black community would only support a mandatory, fixed-assignment plan. Asian community spokespeople were in agreement.

144 *Without a Court Order*

The November 9 motion, however, took some people by surprise, especially members of the Municipal League. Jerry Skutt remembers the day:

My impression going into the meeting at Northgate was that while there was some pressure for DWAC to act, I understood from Dick [Andrews] that it was not appropriate for DWAC to take definitive action at that time. I had understood from the outset that the Core Committee was not to provide definite direction. The Municipal League had understood that two plans were going to go to DWAC.

[At Northgate] I spoke to the inappropriateness of our acting at that time, and when pressed I went into the ideas of clusters [the desegregation approach Skutt had developed]. I remember Ann's question about a backup, but from the nature of the way I was approaching things, it [a backup strategy] really wasn't called for yet. I was not advocating a voluntary system. I was advocating a structure within which any number of desegregation techniques might have been employed. My ideal would have been to cluster two adjacent minority, racially impacted schools and, say, maybe five non-racially-impacted schools, to look closely at the placement of magnets, and do some active recruitment. If some schools didn't make it the first year, it was okay by the Board's resolution. In some cases you would need some sort of assignment-first mechanism [schools which were ninety percent minority].

The Municipal League felt that to act prior to some decent interval after the last community hearing [November 15] would be a slap in the face, undercutting the credibility of the process. When we were told that the superintendent had given directions on the final plan, it distressed me very much. Not more than two weeks prior, we had assurances from the superintendent that he would adhere to the schedule in terms of the community meetings.[14]

At the DWAC meeting Skutt did consider making a substitute motion but decided against the idea. The motion, to the best of his recollection, would have discussed an expanded area or cluster of schools between which students would have transferred. He is convinced that his motion would not have passed even if it had been made.[15]

The term "fixed-assignment" is unique to Seattle and deserves some discussion. According to Andrews, the word was coined by himself in a conversation with Jerry Skutt.

Seattle had in operation during the 1977-78 school year a magnet school plan. During that year, the Magnet Plan was attempting to desegregate schools by setting up specialized programs, primarily in minority impacted schools, and recruiting students to volunteer to attend these schools. The plan was strictly voluntary in its approach to student transfers. Three of the desegregation plans written by the school district for consideration as a citywide desegregation plan were based on this already existing Magnet School Plan. However, in addition to a phase of voluntary student recruitment, additional students would be selected by the district for mandatory assignment to magnet schools if schools were not balanced by voluntary transfers.

The second approach desegregated schools by pairing or triading them, creating an enlarged elementary attendance area including both minority and majority impacted schools. Students from both areas would be assigned to one building for primary grades and another for intermediate grades. Feeder patterns to secondary schools would be readjusted to desegregate them. This was a mandatory desegregation plan, without a voluntary student transfer phase, and mandatory busing was not popular.

Some proponents of a voluntary magnet-type plan believed that it might not be necessary to employ the mandatory backup, thereby avoiding the emotional impact of a mandatory desegregation plan for Seattle.[16]

Board member Don Olson had always avoided using the word "mandatory" because of its emotional overtones. Almost everyone involved in DWAC was also sensitive to the emotional baggage that this word carried with it. Dick Andrews was searching for a word to express what a mandatory plan would do without employing the term "mandatory," and possibly looking for some common ground between the Municipal League's approach to desegregation and the approach preferred by the racial minority groups in Seattle. He used the term "fixed-assignment." To individuals who favored a mandatory approach to desegregation, the term immediately became an exact synonym for "mandatory" desegregation and described the Triad Plan. Jerry Skutt did not understand the term to mean mandatory in the sense of the assignment of one student to one school, but instead understood the term to mean the assignment of a student to a cluster of schools, from which the student could select one to attend — a "fixed *area* assignment." Andrews recalls:

> I coined the word "fixed-assignment" in a conversation with Jerry Skutt on the telephone. When he asked me what I meant by "fixed-assignment," I said that no student would be assigned mandatorily on an individual basis. [Assignments are made by geographic area and classes in the Triad Plan.] Jerry misunderstood the meaning of my statement. He picked up that word and used it with his own definition. Jerry thought that a grade reconfiguration [the Triad Plan] would not fall under the definition of a fixed-assignment. But to me, in the Triad Plan, the individual is not assigned on an individual basis. A class of individuals in the same geographic area receive those assignments. The word was so catchy that everyone picked up on it,

and then Jerry was locked into my definition. To a large degree what happened with the Municipal League was that Jerry was locked into his definition of fixed-assignment, and then Jerry felt that I had deceived him. It was a misunderstanding, and it began the breach between Jerry and I. And then I lost him altogether when I said, "Jerry, I have a choice to make." [At Northgate School in the meeting with planners on November 9.] Then I had the audacity to say about his substitute motion [at the DWAC meeting November 9] that it was foolish for him not to have introduced it.[17]

Skutt's recollection is a little different:

I had used the term "fixed-area assignment." Our discussion centered around some combination of those three words. We agreed that any outcome [plan] would include some sort of assignment by area under the premise that you keep neighborhood groups of children together. We were talking simply about matching up sets of schools. It did not speak to exactly how you would balance within that set. It was really a nonconstraining definition, but would have included the Triad Plan.[18]

To most people on DWAC, the term "fixed assignment" meant the Triad Plan, and DWAC had taken a vote on a "fixed-assignment plan with options." The motion meant that DWAC was recommending that Seattle's desegregation plan would first reassign students to achieve racial balance in the schools. After mandatory reassignments were made, students could take advantage of program options. The motion put DWAC on record as favoring the establishment of grade-reconfigured paired or triaded schools, with readjusted secondary school feeder patterns. The manner in which students could gain access to program options was not specified. Most of DWAC's Core Committee, including the maker of the November 9 motion, wanted program options housed within buildings in the paired and triaded schools, with more than one program available to students in each of these buildings. The final Seattle Plan did not provide for options in this manner. Instead, different options were housed in various paired schools and some schools which were not paired. Students had the opportunity to transfer after their initial assignment was made. This "voluntary backup" was the result of a political compromise, accomplished largely through the efforts of Board member Don Olson and Municipal League President Shan Mullin. Seattle, unlike any other school district in the country, has a mandatory desegregation plan with a voluntary backup.

When the motion at DWAC on a fixed-assignment-first plan with options was passed, the superintendent was leaning in the direction of that approach to desegregation, but probably had not made up his mind entirely. Board members Cheryl Bleakney, Suzanne Hittman and Dorothy Hollingsworth were also discussing a fixed-assignment plan as their preference. The vote, however, determined the direction Seattle would take in its final desegregation plan. The School Board had given the superintendent authorization to bring only one final plan to the Board on November 2. It is extremely unlikely that the Board could have asked for a rewritten plan after receiving the superintendent's and still made the December 15 deadline for adoption of a plan, though minor modifications would be possible. Had the Board not adopted a plan by the deadline, the prospect of a court suit would have still existed.

Needless to say, DWAC's vote on November 9 created some controversy and hard feelings for which Siqueland and the Church Council received criticism.

After the November 9 DWAC motion, the question of who was going to write the Seattle Plan still remained. The desegregation planning staff was divided on the approach to the plan.

The district had been writing "Plan A" in late October, a voluntary-first approach, and this became public knowledge through an article in the *Weekly*, written by David Brewster, that implied that the plan was being hidden from the public. Following the *Weekly* article, Board members looked at "Plan A." Cheryl Bleakney described it as an incomplete plan:

We all got copies of it [Plan A] when it blew up in the paper. I had never seen copies of it before that. But when it blew up in the *Weekly*, we all felt we needed to see a copy. All it was was just the beginning elements. It was working papers, showing schools. It was fairly thick, but it was incomplete. Moberly wanted to see both plans, and then said, "No. Just go with one."[19] We'd already given him the go-ahead to bring us just one plan. He intended to bring us only one, but he just looked at both.[20]

"Plan B" became the Seattle Plan. Having been removed from the desegregation planning office, Dick Dyksterhuis was off by himself in mid-November, thinking. He had been working on simulations for a fixed-assignment plan based on the Urban League's Triad model. In the week of November 14, the superintendent asked him to identify the schools to be paired for the Seattle Plan[21] and to use the Urban League model to write the final plan.

Because the majority of the desegregation planners were so opposed to the fixed-assignment Triad Plan, only Dick Dyksterhuis, Ricky Malone and Patte

Poc (DWAC's secretary who had been employed to help desegregation planners as a DWAC representative) were available to write the final plan. Dick Andrews had continually told DWAC members that they might have to write the Seattle Plan, and in fact, many of them did help write it, by doing the mathematical calculations needed (the computer was not available) as well as writing the narrative. Dick Dyksterhuis is the author of the Seattle Plan, which he wrote with the help of DWAC members under extreme pressure in a very short time.

When the superintendent came to me and asked me to put the schools together for the plan, I had to have it done by the following Monday.[22]

Dyksterhuis had less than a week, including the Thanksgiving weekend. He delivered the plan on Monday, November 21, meeting his deadline. The plan went to DWAC that night. Dyksterhuis's recollection reveals the amount of work to be done in that short period of time.

What I wanted to do was some school closures, boundary changes and pairings all at once, but there had to be some tradeoffs.

We had identified a number of schools, more than we could use, because we wanted to balance socioeconomic factors as much as we could. My concern was to do as much as possible with pairs; triading was out. I was told we could not use a true triad, with two grades per school and students moving to all three. So I wanted to pair. It was hard to find white schools with a large enough population to pair, so we were going to have to consolidate [close] schools.

We suggested closing schools and making boundary changes so I had a sufficient population. For me a sufficient population was twenty percent more white students than would do the job. Every city I've heard about has had a significant departure from the city the first year. There was not twenty percent override in the pairs when the plan was adopted.

I was working with eight area administrators, the associate superintendent, and citizens' groups. There must have been eighteen or nineteen people that I had to attend to.

In the beginning I had every minority school in a pair or split-pair because I wanted to do it all the first year. I wanted to do all the elementary schools the first year. The second year we could pick up the problems with the secondary schools, which I thought would be significant.

To do a perfect job with selecting schools, etc., it would have taken a month. The superintendent had said he had to have the names of the schools involved by Monday.

One of the things I wanted to do was to put [program] options only in paired and split-paired schools.

There were modifications made in the plan. There were no boundary changes, and options and special progams were also placed in schools that were not paired or split-paried.

What you do as a planner is do a simulation which includes boundary changes and some school closures, and then you give it to the superintendent. We had these offstage meetings with the Board, and gave them the numbers [racial percentages], and I guess there wasn't sufficient support to make the boundary changes.

We were going to make the paired schools the best educational environment possible, with flexible programs and good staff. We asked for a fixed-assignment model with the only options located in paired and split-paired schools.

If you were a majority parent or a minority parent, given the proposed boundary changes, etc., there would have been sufficient kids to provide ethnic identity.

I'm strong for equal educational opportunity. That's number one. We've always had some excellent programs for some kids. But we've not had excellent programs for all kids. That bothers me. The public schools are obligated to provide all kids with access to good quality teachers. I saw desegregation as the opportunity to make access to that quality equal.[23]

Dick Andrews recalls his involvement in writing the Seattle Plan.

I went down to the district offices and I said to Dick [Dyksterhuis], "You do the middle section and I'll do the narrative."

I went home and wrote the rest of the plan while Dick worked on the middle section, identifying the schools.

Dick Dyksterhuis initially had paired all the minority impacted schools, but then through that week as we began to look at the numbers, he had to add additional white impacted schools to make split-pairs.

I said I would clear my calendar for the next week, and Arlis Stewart said she would clear her calendar for the next week, and that's when I called Ann Siqueland, Kay Groves, Arlene Oki, Cheryl Crawford and Barbara Beuschlein. They sat in the room across the hall from Dick and rolled the damn numbers forward.

I said to Dick, "Tell me what you want and we will generate the data for you." Everything had to be done by hand. If Dick could have just gone in to the computer people and said, "I want you to run a simulation on doing this school and this school, changing all this around, and gone on with something else, and within an hour have had the data back to look at, it would have been different. But everything that was done was done by DWAC people, sitting across the hall, calculating the racial percentages and the building capacities. Every time Dick made a change, the calculations had to be done by hand.

We were down there on Thanksgiving Day. I took my kids. Barbara [Andrews] happened to be sick on Thanksgiving Day, and that's how I got by with it, because I took the kids.

Don't let anyone pick on my committee, because that is a group of people who are unreproachable in their ethics, their commitment to desegregation, and in their preoccupation with doing what was right. That is what got us a desegregation plan. It was DWAC people who spent Thanksgiving Day down in the school district headquarters, working on that desegregation plan, when the people who were being paid to do it were home enjoying Thanksgiving with their families.[24]

The Seattle Plan was released publicly at DWAC's next meeting, the Monday following Thanksgiving. DWAC officially endorsed the plan in December.

How Dick Dyksterhuis and DWAC members survived the grueling ordeal of writing the final plan remains a mystery. The level of commitment to desegregate Seattle Public Schools with a plan that was "just, right and equitable" was certainly one factor. The toll the effort took on many individuals, emotionally and physically, cannot be assessed, but was considerable.

The plan had been written by November 21. The School Board was scheduled to vote on December 14. The various organizations represented on DWAC went through their own processes to respond to the final Seattle Plan.

CHAPTER 13

COMMUNITY REACTION

A considerable amount of pressure was exerted by Seattle's black community on the school district to adopt a mandatory, fixed-assignment plan. The black community's united position had a determining effect on the structure of the Seattle Plan.

In October of 1977 a coalition of black community groups began to meet regularly to discuss a unified position on the kind of desegregation plan Seattle should adopt. Jerome Page, director of the Urban League, was instrumental in calling together this coalition. On November 16, 1977, Connie Herring made a statement to the School Board on behalf of the coalition. The statement included nine points that the black coalition felt must be included in a comprehensive desegregation plan. Briefly, the statement recommended that:

> a. Any desegregation plan adopted must be based on a fixed assignment strategy. We will not accept any plan based upon voluntary strategies.
>
> b. We cannot support any desegregation plan which does not foster or ensure a sense of community.... Our aim is toward heterogeneity: ethnically, culturally and economically....
>
> c. We recommend that those schools which have traditionally and historically been deemed "minority schools" maintain no less than 50 percent minority enrollment. Where minority students have to transfer to create or impact racial balance, then no less than 34 percent minority students [should] be reassigned to any school ... outside their historic school.... The plan should be fair, just and equitable for black youth.
>
> d. We cannot support any desegregation plan that does not include the participation of kindergarten age students.[1]

e. The middle school program should be maintained . . . the present Magnet/VRT programs be reconstituted . . . to provide quality educational opportunities that all children can enjoy and not for the singular purpose of moving bodies.

f. Eliminate to a great extent the need for program transfers throughout the district . . . [to] control student population within any desegregation plan.

g. *We refuse to give the issue of white flight any credence.* [Emphasis in original.]

h. The plan should include deliberate progress toward racial and socioeconomic heterogeneity in all schools.

i. The issue of bilingual programs should not defuse or detract from the overall issue of desegregation. . . . Dialectic barriers are just as paramount as specific language barriers.[2]

The statement included a description of the staffing needs of schools participating in the plan and expressed the concern that special math and reading skill programs (compensatory education) be retained.

With the exceptions of the inclusion of kindergarten and the outline of a method to provide for educational quality in schools, the recommendations of the black coalition are basically included in the Seattle Plan.

The Central Area School Council endorsed the Seattle Plan on December 7 because of its "fixed assignments, clear feeder patterns and equity of movement."[3]

The NAACP did not endorse the plan, but promised the School Board that it would continue in the role of a watchdog to make certain that the Board followed through on what it said it would do. The statement was made at the first of two public hearings on the final plan, held on December 5. At that hearing, Jerome Page also spoke for the Urban League and urged the School Board to remain committed to the resolutions it passed in June. He said, "I must state that I am pleased with the direction of this plan. . . . Education at any level in a segregated context is not quality education."[4]

In order for a desegregation plan to succeed, it was essential that Seattle's black community support it. The support of city government was also critical. In the spring of 1977, Woody Wilkinson became deputy mayor in Seattle, Shelly Yapp became the deputy director of the Office of Policy Planning, and

Sidney Freeman was promoted to the position Yapp had held, school liaison. In that capacity, Freeman served as the city's representative on DWAC. Between June, when the School Board adopted the resolutions which mandated the development of the Seattle Plan, and December 14, when the Seattle Plan was adopted, Freeman worked with other community group representatives analyzing desegregation strategies and the five planning models, and ultimately analyzing the most effective desegregation plan for Seattle. Both Sidney Freeman and Shelly Yapp participated on the No-Name Committee, as did others from OPP.

During the month of November, discussions regarding the specific desegregation plan the School Board would adopt became intense. At one meeting of the No-Name Committee, Dick Andrews raised the question of whether or not the city had been formally asked to comment on the five desegregation planning models being reviewed by the community. Olaf Kvamme, also in attendance at the meeting, indicated that Sidney Freeman sat on DWAC and had reviewed the plans with that group. Andrews insisted that a formal request from the district should go to the mayor asking that the city do an analysis of the alternative planning models. Kvamme arranged for an official request for the city's opinion to be sent to the mayor. Andrews recalls the process:

What the district did was send a letter that said, "We have these five desegregation models; would you please give your analysis?"

I didn't want another school closure situation with the city standing over there taking potshots at the district, and the district taking potshots at the city. We couldn't afford to have that happen. If the city wanted to change anything about where the planning process was leading, they had to act then, rather than to react to the district.

Olaf Kvamme and I were asked to meet with the staff of OPP because they wanted to get straight just what was being asked. They said, "Now are you asking us to endorse one of the plans?" I said, "No. I don't want you to endorse any one of those five plans, because the final plan probably isn't going to be any one of those models, but talk about the principles in each of the plans and the potential impact on the city."[5]

A letter was delivered to the School Board from the mayor on November 16 outlining three criteria which the city had identified as essential to the final plan. Sidney Freeman recalls the issues involved in the letter:

We analyzed the five models, stressing (1) the need to move neighborhood groups of children together; (2) the need for equity of student movement; and (3) that the plan could be relied on from year to year and parents would know where their children were going to school. This would suggest that we saw fixed-assignment somewhere in the plan.[6]

According to Freeman, the third issue, reliability, was important as "a sort of gut issue for those of us who still had children in school. We wanted to know where they [children] would be going to school each year. Perhaps there was a little bit of, 'Let's get it over and done with, please!' "[7] The letter from the mayor also encouraged the School Board to continue the open process of public discussion of desegregation alternatives.

The letter fell technically short of endorsing a specific fixed-assignment desegregation plan modeled after the Urban League's Triad Plan. However, according to Shelly Yapp, the city understood that the letter could be read as an endorsement of that type of plan.[8] Dick Andrews recalls that he was overjoyed when the letter arrived; it went further than he had ever hoped.[9]

Charles Royer had been elected mayor of Seattle in November and was scheduled to take office the first of January. Arlene Oki, who had been actively involved in Royer's campaign, arranged for an extensive briefing of the mayor-elect. Superintendent Moberly and members of DWAC met with Royer, and Uhlman and Woody Wilkinson also briefed the new mayor. Along with other issues which were addressed during the transition between the administrations of Uhlman and Royer, desegregation also needed the city's attention in order that the public and the school district would know whether or not the new city administration would change the city's position on this issue.

Charles Royer had had some personal experience with the subject of public schools and desegregation. As he recalls:

When I first came to Seattle in 1970 and went to work for KING-TV, I spent a lot of time covering the issue of desegregation and talking about public schools. Partly as a result of that, I became the president of the PTSA at Eckstein Middle School, which was one of the early receiving schools in the desegregation effort [the Middle School Plan]. One thing we did at Eckstein — which was helpful, I think, to the desegregation effort, and which had an impact upon the way I approached it — was that we got parents and teachers together who were sending students to Eckstein to try and work out the problems we had. And we had early problems at Eckstein, big problems. We didn't work out all of them, but we worked out some of them. And the lesson to me was that you have to get parents involved and you have to confront problems head-on and talk rather frankly with one another.

Most people who think the Seattle school system isn't as good as it should be have never been in the schools. People have a perception of problems, but they just haven't been in there. They haven't been in the classroom recently. We got people into the school.[10]

Uhlman had understood clearly that city government had to play a leadership role in desegregation, and had therefore set the city's policy on desegregation for years to come through his efforts. Royer also felt that it was important for him to show strong political leadership on desegregation. As he puts it:

There had to be political leadership, positive political leadership [talking about the need to desegregate]. I felt a responsibility to speak out in favor of the system and the process which resulted in a local decision [to desegregate Seattle Public Schools], unlike the President of the United States [Nixon] who went to Boston and basically said that what the Supreme Court had said didn't matter, what due process suggests doesn't matter, that a decision made in an orderly fashion doesn't matter. He thereby invited resistance, invited violence, invited problems. Political leadership must speak to an orderly decision-making process where everybody has had an opportunity to speak, and say that that decision is a fair decision. Political leaders ought to speak out in favor of that.

You also ought to speak about the higher goals. The need for us, even if we have to do it artificially, to bring people together so they can learn together in a multiracial and multiethnic society. That is a piece of education. I don't care what the academics say, or how many times they repudiate what has been said in the past. The fact is that working together, and getting to know each other at an early age, has to have a benefit to us in the long term. That is the reason we are doing this difficult and wrenching thing. It's a good reason, and a big one. It's hard to get your hands on it to put it down on your coffee table so you can look at it, but it is a big and important thing that we are doing.[11]

A smooth transition between the Uhlman and Royer administrations was conducted. That transition included a joint statement on the proposed Seattle Plan made to the first of the two School Board hearings on that plan, December 5 at the Seattle Center. Woody Wilkinson made the statement for Uhlman and Royer. The statement was both a personal comment from Wilkinson, whose children attended one of the schools paired in the Seattle Plan, and a statement that both mayors Uhlman and Royer were in agreement in their support of the district's desegregation effort:

I am here on behalf of both Mayor Uhlman and Mayor-elect Charles Royer. They have asked me to assure you that City support for school desegregation will continue without interruption as we move from the present administration into the next. . . .

School desegregation is another issue in a long line of issues which we are addressing ourselves. We have had the opportunity to learn from the experiences of other cities. We know that if we pull together we can do the job without outside intervention, without losing the authority which should rest in the hands of local officials. . . .

I want to emphasize again that the City has been behind you from the beginning, is solidly with you still, and will be with you in September. I want to thank you for not taking the easy way out – for having the great courage to do the right thing – for paving the way for all of us who live here to enjoy Seattle's greatest asset – all of its people.[12]

Charles Royer actually endorsed the Seattle Plan after taking office. This move could have helped avoid the possibility that a different desegregation plan might surface later which the city would be asked to endorse. It was necessary to stand firmly behind the Seattle Plan after the School Board adopted it in order that the plan would not lose community support.

Traditionally, staff members of the Chamber of Commerce play an influential role in the activities of the chamber, and Rob Makin played a determining role in the chamber's involvement in desegregation. The chamber's basic approach, according to Makin, was, "We're with you; we're going to support you; but we aren't as concerned with the details."[13]

When the five desegregation models were released for community review in September, Makin recalls that these plans had been developed so quickly that they were received cynically by many in the chamber. Individually, each of the plans was considered to be unacceptable. Creating "zones" within the district to keep transportation distances and costs to a minimum seemed like an obviously good idea (part of Plan IV). The chamber was interested in assuring that the Seattle Plan be cost-effective and also was concerned that the community's attitude toward it be positive. As it became increasingly clear that a voluntary plan with a mandatory backup would require large amounts of district staff time to tabulate the racial percentages and determine the number of students to be mandatorily assigned after a period of voluntary recruitment each year, the chamber became more and more skeptical that a voluntary-first plan could be adequately administered. The chamber's attitude was basically pragmatic: They were interested in a plan that was realistic, but they were not at all interested in socioeconomic desegregation, one of the premises of the Urban League's Triad Plan. The chamber felt that desegregation was a racial, not a socioeconomic, issue. However, by mid-October, Makin recalls that several individuals associated with DWAC and the No-Name Committee could describe the likely structure of the final Seattle Plan, a structure based on paired or triad schools as in the Urban League's plan, and including magnet programs. Makin specifically recalls discussing the structure of the final plan with Dick Andrews in mid-October; the plan they discussed is basically the plan the School Board adopted in mid-December.[14]

Throughout the development of the Seattle Plan, Rob Makin kept Wallace Bunn, president of the chamber's board, informed almost daily about events that were taking place. Bunn probably devoted at least five hours per week to the subject of desegregation while also fulfilling his other responsibilities as president of the chamber and president of the three-state-area Pacific Northwest Bell. Makin's visits with Bunn were so frequent that Makin was allocated a parking slot at Bunn's office. Desegregation was clearly a high priority for Bunn.[15]

As the time approached when a recommendation on the final Seattle Plan would be made, and as the apparent conflict between individuals who favored a "fixed-assignment-first" approach and those who favored a "voluntary-first" approach also surfaced, the chamber remained relatively neutral concerning the type of plan Seattle should adopt, probably in part because there was not unanimity of opinion in the chamber. According to Makin, paired schools were desirable because they provided for efficient transportation and kept students from each community together. At the same time, according to Makin, the chamber also felt that it was essential to keep optional magnet-type programs available. Creating zones would also reduce transportation costs. Wallace Bunn generally shared Makin's views.[16] However, Russ Amick continued to favor a voluntary-first approach to desegregation, as did some others in the chamber.[17]

Rob Makin sometimes became frustrated with the lengthy meetings during which DWAC discussed the shape of the final plan they wished to recommend. Dick Andrews could never be faulted for not providing everyone with an opportunity to have his or her say. And lengthy discussions often resulted in much digression, causing DWAC meetings to last until midnight on many occasions. Unlike some memers of the Municipal League, Rob Makin felt that a motion at DWAC on a recommendation for the Seattle Plan was appropriate as soon as there were sufficient votes for it to pass.[18]

Two days before Superintendent Moberly publicly announced his intention to recommend the Seattle Plan to the School Board, he invited Wallace Bunn, Rob Makin and Russ Amick to his office to explain to them the decision he had made. (The chamber did not know at this time that Moberly had made a decision, and felt that there was still an opportunity to lobby for a voluntary plan with a mandatory backup, according to Amick.) Amick recalls that the chamber members argued strongly for the voluntary-first approach, and describes the discussion as "an argument" which did not change the superintendent's mind. Moberly explained his reasons for making a decision to fix the assignment of students (as in the Triad Plan model); the district's staff could not handle the requirement of recruiting voluntary student transfers before mandatory assignments could be made because this would be a time-consuming process to go through yearly. The fixed-assignment model would be more efficient from an administrative point of view.

While understanding Moberly's reasons for making the decision, Amick still preferred the voluntary-first model. According to Amick, the chamber did not endorse the Seattle Plan because it felt that the plan would not be stable; it would be necessary to readjust attendance areas over time because parents tend to react to a mandatory desegregation plan by moving or sending their children to private schools, which would unbalance the racial percentages in schools.

However, commenting on the entire process for developing the Seattle Plan, Russ Amick says, "It couldn't have been a more public process than it was. CiVIC members must not have been reading the papers and must not have gone to any meetings in their community."[19] Clearly the Chamber of Commerce knew what had been going on and was deeply involved in the decision-making process.

Shan Mullin, president of the Municipal League in 1977, is fond of saying that there were two kinds of people involved in developing a desegregation plan in Seattle: people who were goal-oriented and people who were process-oriented. He goes on to say that the goal-oriented people accomplished their goals, but the process-oriented individuals did not get to finish the process that was set in motion.

Shan Mullin describes himself as a "process person" and describes the Municipal League as the organization most involved with the "process" of developing the Seattle Plan. Mullin saw the need for a process because of his conviction that Seattle would be best served by adopting a desegregation plan which would be acceptable to the most people, and his deep concern to avoid conflict in the city.

A decision-making process had also been outlined by the district. Two primary issues are viewed by Mullin as a violation of that process: The first is the Board's decision on November 2 to have the superintendent bring them one final plan instead of two; and the second is the passage of DWAC's November 9 motion to recommend a plan (before the last community meeting reviewing the five planning models was held on November 15).

A planning schedule included in the five planning alternatives issued in September referred to final desegregation "plans" (plural) to be written by the district, and indicated that the superintendent should recommend to the Board one or more plans. William Maynard's planning schedule of October 26 indicated that the district planners would write two final plans between November 4 and November 11.[20]

On November 2 the School Board directed the superintendent to bring them only one plan. Bill Maynard had prepared a short memo to David Moberly itemizing the problems that would result if the Board received two plans:

> I. If the administrative recommendation and District-Wide Advisory Committee recommendations are the same, we will be accused of developing the second plan as a ruse.
>
> II. If the administrative recommendation is for one plan and District-Wide Advisory Committee recommends the other, the result may well be polarization of the Board and the community.
>
> III. The human resources necessary to fully develop two plans within the timeline are limited and the task extremely difficult.[21]

For these reasons, the School Board elected to receive only one final plan for consideration.

Mullin and the Municipal League, however, felt that this decision prevented the School Board from giving full consideration to the two planning models which were being discussed.

When DWAC voted to recommend a "fixed-assignment-first, with options" desegregation plan, it became extremely unlikely that the voluntary plan with a mandatory backup would receive serious consideration. Mullin had wanted to see a debate on the pros and cons of the two planning approaches (voluntary-first; fixed-assignment-first) by the School Board.[22] He felt he had been assured this would happen and had also promised others worried about possible mandatory desegregation that voluntary-first approaches would be fully considered.

The Municipal League's approach to desegregation is outlined in a November 21, 1977, paper, "Municipal League Position on Desegregation," which says, in part:

The Municipal League prefers a plan which divides the City into four zones of three high school consortia each....

Within the zones, clusters of approximately five elementary schools each could be established, containing one or two minority impacted schools.... The clusters would also establish the feeder patterns for middle schools, junior high schools and high schools....

Within the established clusters, desegregation strategies would be applied to effect the elimination of all racially isolated elementary schools. This could be accomplished by pairing and triading with grade reconfigurations, two or more whole-school magnets, or by other methods. Another means of desegregation within a cluster might be the creation of special programs in two or more schools in the cluster, permitting students within the cluster to select them, and providing one or more mandatory back-up strategies to achieve racial percentages within the schools. A random mandatory assignment would not be the preferred back-up strategy. Entire single grade transfers might be an example of a preferred alternative.

We strongly recommend ... a ... process permitting schools ... to propose to the School Board a workable alternative for their schools of desegregation within the applicable unit suited to their specific circumstances.[23]

On November 17, 1977, Superintendent Moberly invited Shan Mullin and Richard Andrews to a breakfast meeting to tell them what plan he would be recommending to the School Board. Mullin brought Eben Carlson with him to the meeting. Superintendent Moberly described the two plans available to him by writing their characteristics on a napkin, and then drew a circle around the one he was going to recommend. He circled the "fixed-assignment" plan.[24]

Arlis Stewart's reflections on the process which brought about the Seattle Plan address the politics of that effort:

There was a lot of manipulation during the last stage. I would draw the line somewhere around August 1977. Until then, I think people were fairly open, exploring a bunch of alternatives. Prior to August you had a lot of people who expanded their understanding of what was at stake. After August, I saw most of the real manipulations. We knew there was a deadline. We knew that one way or another a decision was going to have to be made, and people started plotting strategies.

When it finally comes down to it, somebody's going to be smarter than somebody else in reaching a political solution (and I think all solutions are political).

One of the strategies was to have DWAC and the Municipal League and the chamber going through the same analysis at the end so that at least they would not disagree over any major demographic or historical data differences. Jerry Skutt wrote the questions that were the basis for that analysis, with Dick Andrews' and my help. It led you right down the primrose path to a pairing strategy. Jerry probably did not realize that.

DWAC, as a bigger, broader group, was saying that it was essential to have the chamber and Municipal League's agreement.

But Jerry had convinced himself that the term "fixed-assignment" meant that you could have a lot more flexibility in zonings and clusters, more flexibility as to how kids got from one school to another school. And at the end he and the Municipal League felt betrayed.

I'm still surprised that the Municipal League went along with the final plan, but they did.[25]

The process whereby students involved in the American Friends Service Committee's Student Action Force on Education (SAFE) developed a position favoring the kind of plan finally adopted by the School Board is interesting because it reflects the kind of process many individuals were engaged in during this time. Frequently, when individuals took the time to seriously weigh the alternatives presented by the various approaches to desegregation Seattle could have taken, they realized that a fixed-assignment or mandatory plan was the best strategy.

Jonis Davis recalls the SAFE discussion about the final desegregation plan:

When the five draft plans came out, we looked at them and the students said, "What is this!" It was a formidable document. I did an analysis of the five models using a "carrot and stick" formula and put it on one page.

Several of the students took the "carrot and stick" paper to classes at their schools, explained it and then asked the class to vote.

The trend was in favor of a strictly voluntary plan. Everyone was thinking of themselves, what they wanted to be able to do. There were some very strong statements in favor of the Triad Plan, but they were definitely in the minority.

It seemed like some more analysis was necessary, and I boiled the comments down to three main values that had been expressed by the students: choice, certainty and fairness. Under these headings I wrote down the main comments we had received.

We used this new paper at a SAFE meeting that went on for two and a half or three hours. It was a sustained and intense discussion.

We recorded the level of agreement or disagreement with each of the statements listed under the three topics. It was clear that you couldn't have all three (choice, certainty and fairness) equally in one plan. To their amazement, the students realized that they favored the fixed-assignment plan. There was concensus on the fixed-assignment approach.

They wrote up their statement and read it to the School Board. We warned them that they were likely to get some criticism. Instead they were pleased that others noticed their statement.[26]

The SAFE students had reached the same conclusion as DWAC and many others.

This same consensus did not exist in Seattle Council PTSA. When DWAC voted on its recommendation on the Seattle Plan, representatives from PTSA — Kay Groves, Susan Wallace and Patte Poc — voted in favor of the motion. The council was not entirely pleased. Sue Wallace remembers the events:

PTA was allowed to have three official representatives on DWAC. Patte [Poc] and Kay [Groves] had been chosen, but they needed a third person, and I got a telephone call from Kay, whom I did not know at the time. I was just a local PTA member in a local school. I don't really know why I was asked, but I wanted to know what my obligations were. Kay gave me to understand that either PTA didn't have a position on desegregation, or if they had one, I'd have no trouble going along with it.

I started going to DWAC in the summer of 1977. I really didn't know very much about desegregation. I knew that we had magnet programs and that we had a middle school mandatory program, but I didn't have any idea where we might be going.

At one of the first meetings I went to, somebody read some statistics that showed how many schools were out of balance and that we were getting more [segregated] instead of less.

At first the magnet program seemed appealing. But I went on a couple of school visits to evaluate the magnet programs. I saw programs that were very expensive and served only a small percentage of a school population, and those kids seemed to be totally isolated from the rest of the school. I also found out what kind of student movement we were getting and I became convinced that magnets were not going to do as much as we needed to do [to desegregate].

I listened to the five plans the district put forward and in the voluntary-first plans, kids didn't move together. Brothers and sisters wouldn't necessarily go to school together. I felt everyone would live in fear of that kind of instability.

About the end of October, I started to get a picture of what the two alternatives were [a voluntary-first plan or a fixed-assignment plan]. The reason I voted in favor of the fixed-assignment plan [at DWAC] was that I was absolutely convinced we had to do something, and I thought fixed-assignment had the best chance of equity of student movement and stability — the two things that I became convinced were important both from the point of view of all the kids that I supposedly represented and from my point of view as a parent.

But after the DWAC vote, there was a meeting called specifically to deal with the PTA representatives on DWAC. Some people [on PTSA Council] were upset about how the PTA representatives voted. I was asked why I voted the way I did and what my relationship was to PTA. That's when I found out about the fourteen-point PTA position. My vote did agree with that position except for number one, which had to do with using voluntary means first. But I didn't think you could do it [desegregate Seattle's schools] with voluntary means. From that point on I was asked to "follow the rules," and that's why there was a long series of abstentions on votes at DWAC by Kay, Patte and me.[27]

Wallace continued to feel that it was important for PTSA Council to support the implementation of the Seattle Plan and developed a series of suggestions that local PTSA units could use in their own community. The document she developed got her in more hot water.

I sat down and off the top of my head wrote three or four pages of ideas of things to help the local PTAs deal with the issue [of desegregation], and I did write it from the point of view of someone supporting desegregation. It could have been construed as an endorsement of the plan, though I hadn't intended it that way. I had expected that it would be an in-house document that the executive board would mull over and form a committee to do something about. But the executive board decided to mail it out to every local school.

The next PTA Council meeting was just an absolute zoo because people viewed the document as an endorsement of the Seattle Plan.[28]

The council voted to adopt the document, probably because building principals, who are officially members of council, were called by the administration and asked to attend the meeting and support the recommendation.

It is not possible to say that PTSA Council endorsed the Seattle Plan. It is possible to say that members of the council worked to implement the plan. Judith Youngman chaired the effort and was responsible for implementing many of the ideas contained in Wallace's paper, including recruiting bus stop monitors for the first day of school, and encouraging paired school communities to meet together and develop newsletters to keep parents regularly informed about what was happening.

Other groups also endorsed the plan, including the Church Council of Greater Seattle and fourteen regional church denominational heads with offices in Seattle, and the League of Women Voters.

Some modifications were made in the plan that Dick Dyksterhuis and others wrote over the Thanksgiving weekend. No boundaries were changed and no schools were closed to add white populations to the pairs and split pairs (school closure requires the district to develop an environmental impact statement; insufficient time existed to complete that process). Some minority impacted schools were not paired if the Board felt that they could be desegregated by voluntary student transfers only. Specialized options (magnet-type)[29] were also located outside pairs and split pairs, which caused shifts in racial percentages and lower student enrollment in the pairs. However, the Seattle Plan was basically the result of Dick Dyksterhuis's incredible effort. Some people feel that the unresolved issues on desegregation in Seattle are the result of not adopting all components of the plan as Dyksterhuis wrote it. Maintaining racial balance and keeping population size sufficient in some pairs has been a problem.

A review of newspaper coverage of this period indicates when most people in Seattle became aware of what the Seattle Plan would look like.

Beginning in the middle of October, the *Seattle Times* reported that DWAC recommended, among other things, that kindergarten be excluded from the plan. (The School Board adopted this recommendation on December 8.) On November 9, DWAC voted eighteen-to-seven to favor a fixed-assignment-first plan to prevent educational inequality and the need to recruit students each year, and to keep neighborhood groups of students together. The *Times* reported that DWAC took the vote in response to a request from district planners who needed direction. On November 10 the *Times* also reported that a group of parents were afraid of the loss of specialized magnet programs if a triad-type plan was adopted. The School Board received the report on the survey conducted at the thirty community meetings on November 15, indicating the order of preference for the voluntary-first planning models.

On November 16, in a *Times* interview, William Maynard indicated that he felt that the best plan would be a fixed-assignment plan with options. That same day the parents of students in the magnet programs indicated that they wanted magnet programs to continue, and a polling of the School Board revealed that Bleakney and Olson favored a fixed-assignment plan with options, and that Hittman wanted more information. Hollingsworth and Roe were out of town. On November 17 the *Times* reported that the Board members had been edgy at their meeting the day before, realizing that they were scheduled to adopt a plan in less than a month, and that the parents of students enrolled in magnet programs were feeling betrayed. On November 18 and 19 the *Times* reported that Moberly was directing his planners to write a mandatory, fixed-assignment-first plan with options, to do some minor boundary changes and to look at each segregated building individually.

On November 22, the *Times* reported that the "fixed-assignment with options" Seattle Plan had gone to DWAC the night before; on the twenty-third, DWAC's minority report went to the School Board (written by those preferring a voluntary-first plan). A polling of the School Board printed in the *Times* on Novembr 26 indicated that Bleakney and Hollingsworth favored the fixed-assignment plan, Hittman and Olson almost favored it, Sutton was undecided, Alexander was leaning away from the plan, and Roe was absolutely against it. The Board appeared less favorably disposed toward the plan at its meeting on November 28, with Olson indicating that he would vote for a voluntary-first plan, unless the fixed-assignment one contained more options.

While still preferring the fixed-assignment-first plan, Moberly indicated on November 28 that the plan was being rewritten to display the options better. This change was being made to accommodate Don Olson and Shan Mullin of the Municipal League, who felt the plan was too stringent. As Olson said:

I think Shan Mullin's reaction and mine were almost identical, when we first saw the Seattle Plan [after November 21]. We were appalled. He and I worked very closely for the next three weeks to get some flexibility. What I had envisioned was a whole group of magnets, and John Jones out there could go to School X or three other schools where there were magnets. He had a choice. It didn't matter that one of his choices was not to continue at his old school. That choice was closed to him. But he did have the choice of, say, four other schools. That's the way I wanted it, not the way it was in the original plan. That plan didn't have any options. The option was to go to one school, period [the school in the pair]. No other school. That was Shan's and my understanding. There were precious little or no options.

There wasn't any point in holding those citizens' meetings unless you were going to listen to what they had to say. As a practical matter, what the citizens had to say

166   *Without a Court Order*

didn't have very much of a part in what finally came out. It was clear that the citizens wanted only voluntary student movement.

I was surprised by the Seattle Plan. Back in January the instructions given by the superintendent had been for voluntary student movement only. I didn't expect a 180-degree flip. I expected something in between. I had stayed away through the summer months. I hadn't been a part of what was going on in line with the agreement that all Board members had made with each other.

I opposed getting into two armed camps and fighting it out, whatever the context of the fight — in the courts, the headlines of the papers, or whatever.

Between November 22 and December 14 there was a major effort, and Shan and I were probably the ringleaders. We got some changes made. We got a couple of pairs dropped. We tried to get one other one dropped. If that period had been another month or two, I think we would have been able to accomplish more.[30]

When the individual schools to be involved in the Seattle Plan were made public on November 21 at a DWAC meeting, public reaction to the mandatory plan began. One parent in a school pair protested, saying, "My children aren't going to go!" Another paired school indicated that it preferred a court battle. At another school a campaign was begun by white parents to identify their children as black on school records to prevent that school's involvement.

On December 2 the final narrative draft of the plan was scheduled to be released to the press. The superintendent was at a meeting in Spokane (in eastern Washington), and his plane was delayed by a snowstorm in Montana. The narrative of the draft written by Dick Andrews had been rewritten by a member of the administration at Moberly's request to edit out what the superintendent called, "Sociology 101 words." That draft was a "watered-down" narrative[31] and DWAC was upset.

School principals and the press were waiting in the school district's administration offices to receive the final draft. Almost everyone left that night without seeing the plan. Constantine Angelos, *Seattle Times* education editor, described the night in an article appearing the next day, December 3, saying that the final plan "went through prolonged labor pains," and "delivery won't be until sometime today." The article described Moberly, the attending physician, as arriving late for the delivery, and characterized DWAC members standing by as "midwives." What Angelos did not know was that the midwives were in the process of writing another draft of the desegregation plan. DWAC members used the original draft, plus additional information, to revise the administration-written version. A new "cut-and-paste" version of the narrative of the plan was in Dick Andrews' hands when the superintendent finally arrived from Spokane. Andrews took that version in to the superintendent, where it was compared to the administration revision. As Andrews recalls:

When the full-blown plan came out [November 21] with all of the narrative, there was a lot of talk about socioeconomic desegregation. Moberly asked a member of the administration to go over it and eliminate all the "Soc 101 words," and get rid of all the excess verbiage.

I got a call [on December 2] from Bill Maynard saying, "They've massacred the plan!" So I went down there [to the district offices] and got it and read it. I was so mad. After we had spent all that time over the Thanksgiving weekend writing it, and here comes this "abstract" that reduced it to nothing. That's when I called the Core Committee.

The superintendent was in Spokane. And he was going to approve the plan that Friday, and whatever he approved was going to be it.

I also called Cheryl Bleakney. She came down and looked at what had been done and got so mad.

Arlis Stewart, Jerry Skutt, Ann Siqueland and Cheryl Crawford worked in Bill Maynard's office and cut and pasted from the administrative revision and from what DWAC had written before, plus adding some additional things. It was all cut and pasted together and typed. I did not participate in the recutting and writing. I was orchestrating the political atmosphere.

Maynard went into Moberly's office to talk about the administration revision of the plan.

I remember Ann saying, "Are you going to take that cut-paste job in to the superintendent?" And I said, "You bet!" And I walked into Moberly's office and he said, "All right. So we have to have all this Soc 101 stuff." I said, "This plan has been massacred." He said he didn't want to hear what the Urban League and the Church Council were saying. I said, "This draft was written by the Urban League and the Church Council and the Municipal League." Jerry Skutt was there.

It was something like 4:30 or 5:00 and Moberly had a dinner engagement at 6:00.

And Moberly said, "What do you have?" And I said, "We have a different draft for you. I think it picks up the good things in the original draft and the good things in the revised draft. For example, the revised draft has a section that is completely out of place." The section was misplaced. Then Moberly said, "I don't have time to deal with a whole rewrite of that draft; this one's ready to go [the new cut-paste draft]. I'll go with it."

Peggy Moberly had called Dave and asked what kind of wine to serve for dinner. So Dave told her what wine, and finally he said, "That's it!" He left in all the historical stuff, the bilingual stuff, multiethnic curriculum, staff training, in-building segregation, all that stuff. I was utterly amazed because Maynard hadn't even seen some of that, and he played it very nice during the whole review. Moberly read all those things and said, "Now, Bill, you can deliver all this by this day?" And Bill said, "Yeah, I think so."

So there was one copy of the plan. I didn't hand it to Maynard or anyone. I walked out of the office with it. I was delighted to see that everyone was still there.

And Gus Angelos [*Seattle Times* education editor] was there wanting to know where Eric Nalder [*Post-Intelligencer* reporter] was. He was pacing around saying, "Where's Nalder?" He just knew he was going to read about the plan in the morning in the *P.-I.* And I was standing there talking to Gus with the only copy of the plan in my hand. That's when Gus wrote that "midwife" article, which was a brilliant article.[32]

Despite the effort on the night of December 2, and despite the fact that the first final draft of the plan was the one that Dick Andrews convinced the superintendent to use, the narrative of the plan was again rewritten with editorial changes made by Shan Mullin and Don Olson, specifically to remove the statements about in-building segregation, as well as much of the information written the night of December 2 by DWAC's Core Committee.

On December 5 and 6 the School Board held two hearings on the Seattle Plan, the written, rewritten, rewritten, rewritten Seattle Plan. The first hearing was at the Seattle Center and the first part of the hearing was carried live on Channel 9, Seattle's public television channel. Approximately five hundred people attended. The newspapers reported that different individuals tabulated counts on those speaking for and against the plan. Proponents of the plan counted twenty-four speeches favoring the plan, with twenty-two opposing it. Opponents said twenty-one people had favored the plan, with twenty-two opposing it.[33] Proponents of the plan called it the fairest possible, while opponents talked about the breakup of neighborhood schools, the loss of school volunteers and white flight. The first fourteen speakers favored the plan. These speakers were the ones who appeared on the TV coverage. Community organizations familiar with the process for testifying before the School Board signed up before the night of the hearing, having been told by Arlis Stewart that the first part of the hearing would be televised.

The second hearing was held in the southeast area of Seattle at Mercer Junior High and was attended by about 450 people. Again, many people spoke in favor of the plan and many against. But this hearing was most characterized by the large number of non-English-speaking Asian students at the meeting who addressed the School Board in their native language and asked to be excluded from the plan. The plight of Seattle's Asian immigrant population in relation to desegregation was graphically demonstrated at that hearing.

Suzanne Hittman recalls the confusion of immigrant Asian parents which she discovered through meeting with small groups of them that year.

I sat with those bilingual parents in their living rooms at night and worked with interpreters and tried to explain it to them. They absolutely could not understand it [desegregation]. I used to get to the point where I would say to the interpreter, "Tell them I don't understand it either. I don't understand what we are doing. They're just going to move." These were the times when I didn't want to do it [desegregate].[34]

CHAPTER 14

DECEMBER 14, 1977

On December 14, 1977, the seven Seattle School Board members sat down at their podium in the school district's central office building and voted on the Seattle Plan. Patt Sutton arrived from the hospital with a hospital name tag on her arm. The room was filled with about 150 people, most of whom had been working day and night for at least nine months to reach this day. After a brief discussion and statements by Board members, the Board secretary read the names of the Board members for a roll call vote on the motion made by Dorothy Hollingsworth to adopt the administrative guidelines for the Seattle Plan. Most members of the audience knew how the Board would vote, and it seemed somewhat anticlimactic that it took so little — the word "aye," uttered by six individuals — to end public school segregation in Seattle. But that is what it took. That and a lot more. There were tears that day, and relief, and joy, and disappointment, and exhaustion. But it had been done.

The school district had been in court that morning, defending the Board's right to take that vote, in response to a suit filed by individuals who later organized Citizens for Voluntary Integration (CiVIC) to oppose the Seattle Plan. The court had permitted the vote to be taken by denying the CiVIC motion. That would be only the beginning of the discussion of the Seattle Plan in court.

Much has been said by School Board members (and others) about the Seattle Plan before and after December 14. But the comments Board members made that day reflect the core of these individuals' feelings about eliminating segregation in Seattle.

Cheryl Bleakney decided to add her support to the majority of the Board who had extended Superintendent Moberly's contract for another year the previous September.

I want to make a statement in answer in part to some of the criticism which has been leveled at Dr. Moberly. Some statements have referred to the Seattle Plan as the "Moberly Plan." I think we need to make it very clear that Dr. Moberly has been under the firm direction of the Seattle School Board in developing this plan, that he was operating under the two resolutions which were adopted by this Board on June 8 . . . , working under criteria which we gave to him. . . . . I would like to ask your special indulgence to change and add my vote to the vote of the Board members taken last September in extending the superintendent's contract an additional year.[1]

Next, Dick Alexander spoke:

I think many people do not fully realize that there has been a lot of compromising within this Board to get a plan out. . . . I knew that this is probably a very difficult decision for many of us to make, but I think in the long run, the buck really stops with us. . . . We are going to have to make those decisions, not for the best interests of the Board members or the superintendent but for the best interests of kids, for the long run and the health of the city. I think that all has to be found within our plan.[2]

Dorothy Hollingsworth followed:

Knowing that this is not perfect, the opportunity is here for us as elected officials to discharge our duties and responsibilities in upholding the constitution of the State of Washington as well as the United States.[3]

Ellen Roe was sad:

I would like to say that today is a sad day to me and to many supporters of the Seattle Public Schools.

In some backcourt maneuvers, groups threatened legal action if the Board didn't promise to declare a short two-year time limit on desegregating *all* of our schools. In June, Resolution 1977-8 was passed and the "die was cast" with very few people in town realizing what had happened. An unrepresentative desegregation advisory committee and a planning staff started working on proposals. Never did I doubt that it would be a restrictive mandatory plan that would be presented to us, prioritizing social issue and social engineering over education.

Unfortunately, leaders of some groups and many individuals did not realize they could not significantly change a plan written by people with such a sense of urgency and commitment. I believe, in fact, people, including civic leaders, were deceived by the world "voluntarily." Little did they realize, nor would they accept, that the Board meant, "voluntarily desegregating Seattle schools by mandatory strategies. . . ."

The newspapers have urged unanimity on this Board but I cannot and will not support a plan that violates my own personal code and violates the expressed wishes of the majority of the citizens of our city.[4]

Suzanne Hittman:

Thirteen months ago . . . I stated to my fellow Board members that I felt Seattle could desegregate its school district voluntarily and by that I meant without any intervention from any court system. That indeed is the significant step we are taking today. . . .

I think the greatest cost that Seattle could bear would be to not desegregate its schools. The expense there is in raising another generation of children who do not have the opportunity to have an education with all children in the school district is too great. They will not live or learn in the world that is the real world.[5]

Patt Sutton spoke next. Sutton's struggle over her vote had been carried out in a hospital bed. Stress had probably helped put her there.

Eight years, one month and three days ago I sat in the audience as the School Board announced the desegregation of Seattle Public Schools. Today we have twice as many schools which could be considered racially isolated. But we have come a very long way. Community attitude has swung about, racial integration in the classroom is viewed as a desirable goal for every child.

Representation is an enormously complicated responsibility. Sometimes one can try to assess community sentiment and vote that way. In a few instances, and this is one, the elected person puts in weeks and months and years just gaining information on a serious and complicated issue. The person listens and listens to the community and then, in the loneliest situation I have ever faced, one projects the outcomes. The outcomes that I see are not that everything stays the same or forced busing. Nothing will ever be quite the same again. . . .

We have heard much from those opposed to the plan. I have personally spoken with many. These people are not racist; they sincerely believe that what we are about to do is a grievous error of judgment.

A much larger group has received little notice except as their spokespersons have read brief statements. These thousands of people have sat as groups all over this city, probably a bit fearful of impending change, probably annoyed that public schools have been singled out as the trailbreaker of national policy. Each coming from their own starting place, they have ended in quiet, firm support.

Slaying a dragon or casting a vote is a very quick thing . . . but it takes a special kind of courage to face an unexpected dilemma each day in a rapidly changing situation. You have that courage and that is what makes our city great and what will guarantee fine education to all the city's children.[6]

Finally, Board President Olson expressed his concern about flexibility and options in the plan:

This plan as it has finally evolved and as it exists today has all the flexibility of the voluntary proposals that were made in the last few months. . . . The way this plan is evolved there is a possibility for every student in the Seattle school district to exercise an educational option next year for an educational program.[7]

The vote followed with six Board members voting "aye," one "nay."

And so the Seattle School Board had adopted the administrative guidelines for a desegregation plan which paired elementary schools, sending the student bodies of both attendance areas to one of the two schools for grades one, two and three, and to the second school for grades four, five and six. The desegregation of junior highs, middle schools and high schools was phased in, by changing several of the "feeder patterns" for students entering the lowest grade in each of these secondary schools.

Between December 14, 1977, and March 1978, paired-school communities had time to develop plans for their individual schools, including the option to change the grade configuration (which school would house grades one, two, and three, and which would house grades four, five and six) and to select the program options they wished. This community review came about largely through the work of the Municipal League. Between December and March the structure of the Seattle Plan remained the same; however, the feeder patterns for two pairs and triads were readjusted, and other technical changes were made in the plan. These changes might best be characterized as "fine-tuning." The period gave communities which were involved in pairs and triads an opportunity to begin working together. In March, School Board action defined the specific program location, feeder patterns and grade configuration of the schools involved in the plan.

The day the School Board adopted the administrative guidelines for the Seattle Plan — December 14, 1977 — will always be a significant date to DWAC members. Dick Andrews recalls his feelings that day:

We were successful in doing what we did because we put so much time and energy into what we did, and we transferred that energy into our respective organizations.

I had to keep DWAC moving in order to protect my investment. I had invested so much time and energy, so much of my personal reservoir of resources, that I had to win. I couldn't lose it. To have lost on December 14 would have been personally catastrophic. I had to exhaust every ounce of energy. I had to make sure we got the plan. And that's why December 14 was such a joyful, even tearful, occasion. It was such a tremendous emotional drain of energy on the part of organizational leadership on DWAC, including myself, that we had to do everything to win.[8]

Dick Andrews's leadership abilities made it possible for DWAC to win and for the Seattle Plan to be adopted. DWAC members worked, and Dick Andrews provided the leadership to focus DWAC's energy effectively.

DWAC did not disband after December 14, 1977. It continued to meet until March 1981, monitoring the Seattle Plan, and keeping the need for the plan before the School Board as that body made other decisions which affected the plan.[9] The long nights and weekends of work are basically over, and many once hard-working members later put in only an occasional appearance at a Monday night meeting. However, the years of working together have developed bonds of friendship between the members of DWAC that will probably continue until all have snow-white hair.

Each member of DWAC, upon reflecting on what they helped bring about, is aware of some limitations in the Seattle Plan. Each, probably, has had moments of wondering whether he or she really wanted to desegregate schools, because of the trauma such a change produces in the lives of numerous people. Each holds out the hope that the next generation, graduating from Seattle Public Schools, will be not only equipped academically to succeed in the world, but will have gained sufficient firsthand experiences relating to individuals who are racially and culturally unlike themselves — as well as like themselves — that they will also be able to succeed in a pluralistic world. It will be at least twenty years before the fruit of the December 14, 1977, Seattle School Board decision to desegregate the public schools can in any way be evaluated. Someday the children of DWAC members and their contemporaries will be the ones to judge whether the Seattle Plan did make Seattle a more just, right and equitable city in which to live. That certainly was their parents' intent.

Community comment on the plan continued through its adoption. On December 14, 1977, in a letter addressed to Board president Don Olson, the Municipal League supported the administrative guidelines for the Seattle Plan (Resolution No. 77-28), the day the School Board adopted that resolution. The Municipal League's reservation concerned an item in the Board's resolution which appeared "to favor with educational options those students who are in paired and triaded schools."[10] The Municipal League urged the "adoption of a district administrative policy, which provides positive educational options for all students."[11] The final Seattle Plan did that.

While the Seattle Plan was not entirely consistent with the ideas set forth by the Municipal League, that civic organization did have a significant impact on the plan through modifications made in the original draft of the plan.

In reflecting on what happened in Seattle, Shan Mullin recalls:

I never personally saw a voluntary desegregation plan with a mandatory backup strategy that I thought would work. I don't think one was ever developed. My disappointment was that we didn't devote the energies and efforts in trying to do that. There wasn't enough time. There weren't enough people involved. And so we ended up with a plan that I think was perhaps unfortunate. I had hoped, from a political point, we could have developed a plan that would have avoided Initiative 350 or any of those kinds of things — one that we could get everybody behind. I felt that a voluntary plan with a backup would get more support and produce less turmoil. I might be kidding myself.

I have never suggested, however, that I thought we made a mistake. We definitely did the right thing. The only reservation I have is that the process did not match up to my expectation, and the plan which was adopted had some features which could have been better.[12]

Whether Seattle could have avoided the turmoil of defending the Seattle Plan in federal court after the passage of State Initiative 350 (which was aimed at undoing the Seattle Plan by prohibiting the assignment of students beyond their next nearest school), with a different, but still effective, desegregation plan, is a question that can never be answered.

Mullin's frustration with the decision on the Seattle Plan was expressed frequently enough that one meeting of the No-Name Committee was called to discuss "what the Municipal League is up to, if anything."[13] Mullin had expressed his desire for a more voluntary approach to desegregation before and after December 14, and the No-Name Committee provided the opportunity for representatives of other organizations to discuss Mullin's reservations with him face-to-face. The committee had served its purpose.

One summation of the importance of the Seattle Plan was made during the trial concerning the constitutionality of Initiative 350.

Seven prominent black leaders in Seattle made a joint statement on April 23, 1978: Fred E. Stevens (Pastor of First A.M.E. Church), Meredith Mathews (Regional Executive of Pacific Region YMCAs), Lacy Steele (President of the Seattle Branch NAACP), Samuel McKinney (Pastor of Mt. Zion Baptist Church and founder of Seattle's Opportunities Industrialization Center), Larry Gossett (Director, Central Area Motivation Program), Jerome Page (President/Executive Officer, Seattle Urban League), and Charles Z. Smith (Professor of Law and past Associate Dean of the Law School at the University of Washington).

We support the Seattle Plan because it fulfills the Seattle School Board's June 8, 1977, resolution to desegregate Seattle's public schools and because the plan is equitable. Historically in Seattle the burdens of reducing segregation have fallen disproportionately on blacks. The Seattle Plan, with its pairing and triading of schools and its movement of entire neighborhoods by bus, is the only way to ensure equity of movement, that is, minority and white students sharing equally the inconvenience of busing. This equal sharing had to be a part of the plan for the black community to accept and support it. An additional advantage of the plan is that the movement of entire neighborhoods helps to maintain neighborhood cohesiveness, which is important to blacks in the city.

We feel qualified to state that the Seattle School Board's action to voluntarily desegregate the public schools without court or federal agency compulsion is beneficial to this community because it shows the extent of the Board's commitment to an equitable desegregation plan, it raises the black community's trust in a public institution, the School School Board, and it helps to create a healthy civic climate for blacks.

Further, we feel qualified to state that if Initiative 350 is implemented and the Seattle Plan is thereby dismantled, the response of the minority community — especially the black community — could well be to not participate in a voluntary busing program. Many blacks would consider the implementation of Initiative 350 to be the white community's outright rejection of equitable public school desegregation. Many blacks would turn their attention and energy to neighborhood minority schools and the result would be a highly segregated public school system.

The immense expense and substantial delay resulting from a trial of a desegregation lawsuit brought against the School District would place a tremendous burden on the black community. Housing and employment are also segregated in Seattle (as the schools would be but for the Seattle Plan) and health and welfare programs are often racist. The black community is making a concerted effort to end segregation and racism in all forms in this community. A major desegregation lawsuit would substantially detract from efforts in those other major areas of concern.

The Seattle Plan is the result of a political determination in Seattle that the public schools should be desegregated without court or federal agency intervention. The important black political and education goal of desegregated public schools has been realized in Seattle through the local political process. If Initiative 350 is implemented in Seattle (*i.e.*, the Seattle School District does not assign students to other than their nearest or next nearest schools to reduce racial imbalance), these black political and educational gains would be irretrievably reversed. Not only would the Seattle Plan be dismantled and the public schools resegregated, but future school board action to desegregate the schools (except under court order) would be precluded. The realization of the black political and educational goal of desegregated schools at the local school board level would be impossible, no matter what the local political concensus is and no matter how educationally beneficial school desegregation is.

To date, the Seattle Plan has not been reversed.

The ACLU did not discuss proposed desegregation plans under review in Seattle in the fall of 1977 in much detail, and never recommended that Seattle adopt a specific plan. In fact, Dan Levant felt the Seattle Plan was far more extensive than he personally would have liked:

> The problem now is living with the results of our action. I want to make it clear that I didn't have any plan in mind. I don't think busing is a very good idea. I just think that maintaining the status quo was a worse idea, and I think the plan we have is as good as we could have had, but I'm bothered by it. It's manipulation of people. I never felt we had to desegregate to this degree – to this extent. My target was to remove the extremes of segregation, particularly in elementary schools.[14]

At one point or another, almost every person involved in the effort to end segregation in Seattle, even those who were most adamant in their desire, has felt the burden of knowing the amount of disruption desegregation causes for Seattle public school children and their families. Dan Levant is no different. Change is painful, and even in those individuals who were instrumental in bringing about change, there is the desire to avoid that pain. But there were also other feelings associated with the ACLU's effort to desegregate Seattle Public Schools. David Harrison recalls:

> There is nothing that I did in the five years that I worked for the American Civil Liberties Union that I feel was more important than my work on desegregation. I think that ACLU played a unique role. That role was crucial, and that the end result is something that Seattle can be very proud of. I wish all stories had the same end – the same happy ending. As far as I'm concerned, it is a happy ending . . . or at least a happy beginning.[15]

Sam Shoji kept the Japanese American Citizens League informed regularly about desegregation planning in process during 1977 and on. While JACL never officially took a vote endorsing the Seattle Plan when the School Board adopted it in December, its support was later expressed when the group filed a brief of amicus curiae on the side of the school district in its fight to have State Initiative 350 declared unconstitutional.

One of the few DWAC meetings attended by Gary Higashi was the November 9, 1977, meeting in which DWAC voted to recommend a desegregation plan that was "fixed-assignment-first with options." At the public hearings on the plan held by the School Board in December, Higashi read a statement from the Asian American Education Association endorsing the Seattle Plan.

It would have been possible for spokespeople from the Asian community in Seattle, or organizations from the various Asian communities, to oppose Seattle's desegregation effort. This did not happen. A few active individuals, working very hard, had participated in the debate over a plan for Seattle, successfully keeping others informed of the issues which concerned Asians, and at the same time informing the general Asian population about what was happening in desegregation planning. Seattle points with pride to the fact that its civic and business leadership supported desegregation efforts, thereby minimizing open opposition and divisiveness over desegregation. The same thing can be said about the participation of active members of the Asian community. They were effective in communicating concerns of the Asian community, in participating in decisions which were made, and in providing visible leadership for the larger Asian community.

Both mayors Uhlman and Royer feel positive about Seattle's decision to desegregate its public schools voluntarily. Uhlman says:

I am pleased with the results [of my involvement in desegregation], and I'm happy with my role. It was one of the decisions you make as mayor that you gain a great deal of satisfaction from. When you can point to something you have done that has had an influence on a community, it gives you satisfaction. Desegregation was like the satisfaction that I gain when I walk through Pioneer Square [the oldest part of Seattle, which was renovated during Uhlman's administration]. It would not have been there if I hadn't been there to make the decisions and the differences. Desegregation is not as concrete (if you will excuse the pun) as Pioneer Square, or a waterfront aquarium or a waterfront park, but nevertheless, it is every bit as important, or more important. Because desegregation affects the social fabric of this city.

I personally have a prejudice. I do not believe that any one inner-city school district can succeed in the battle against school desegregation alone. It's impossible. That's why I made that initial proposal [the Luther Burbank interdistrict plan] years ago, and I still stand by it. I believe that if we're going to solve the problem of inner-city school segregation, we're going to solve it by bringing in the suburbs. It can realistically be brought about by a court order. Our "voluntary" plan was adopted at the point of a gun. And that gun can point at five districts, just as easily as it can point at one. It will never happen voluntarily. It can realistically be brought about through a court order. If a court says to three or five or seven districts, "You must get together or else the court will take jurisdiction and appoint a master who will run the schools," it could happen.[16]

History will record whether or not Seattle will ever be involved with the surrounding school districts in a metropolitan desegregation plan, but the possibility exists.

Royer reflects on the significance of "local control" to the decision-making process in Seattle, and on the related issues of facilities and quality education.

We did it locally and that was the key. Local control in Seattle is almost a religion. We did it [desegregated] for some excellent and noble and good reasons.

The School Board has a big tough responsibility. If we had been able to settle some of the problems with school facilities and been able to address the rampant public concern about the quality of education before we took that big step [to desegregate schools], that would have been much better. I still don't know whether the School Board could have done this or not.

I still think it was the right decision. A decision of which the School Board can be proud. An awfully hard decision. There just isn't any tougher decision, but one that was done locally within our own rules. I think it was in the overall best interest of the city.[17]

After the Fourteenth

The level of exhaustion experienced by individuals who were deeply involved in the community organizing and strategizing to bring about the Seattle Plan, as well as in the plan's actual writing, could have best been observed at a meeting held at Dick and Barbara Andrews's home in May of 1978. The meeting was the first attempt to organize opposition to proposed Washington State Initiative 350, then being circulated for signatures by Citizens for Voluntary Integration. Many members of DWAC as well as other individuals involved in the community organizations which supported the plan were present, along with three members of the School Board. It was a warm spring evening and the Andrewses had provided wine and crackers and cheese for the evening.

Cheryl Bleakney attempted to chair the meeting, and through no fault of hers, almost nothing was accomplished. No one was able to take the business at hand seriously. Jokes were made about every idea suggested for the campaign. Several individuals retired to the porch. With the exception of the League of Women Voters representative, who was developing a packet of information for a state convention, little energy appeared to be available to fight the initiative.

It is doubtful that an outside observer would believe that the individuals in the Andrews living room that evening had the capacity to organize their way out of a paper bag, let along organize support for the first comprehensive desegregation plan brought about in a major American city without a court order. But these individuals had done just that. However, on that warm evening in May, they were too exhausted to take anything else seriously.

One of the flaws in Seattle's planning effort was the absence of a planned-for backup of fresh, energetic individuals available to take over when others were exhausted. With a few exceptions, community organizing had not reached the local neighborhood level, and no new troops were available when the old guard ran out of steam. And run out they did.

That was the last time wine was served at a meeting concerning Initiative 350. The campaign, however, lacked energy throughout. Few people had the capacity to climb one more hill. Initiative 350 passed in the state of Washington by a two-to-one margin. While it is likely that the initiative would have passed anyway, the lack of energy of the organized opposition to it was also a factor.

Dick and Barbara Andrews hosted an intentional party for DWAC, school district personnel and others in June. It was a much-deserved celebration. The Andrews home was a perfect place for the celebration. It had been the site of many meetings of DWAC subcommittees, and many of the ideas included in the Seattle Plan developed there.

If Seattle schools were desegregated with the aid of a "handbook" on how to do the job well, that handbook was an August 1976 report of the U.S. Commission on Civil Rights, *Fulfilling the Letter and Spirit of the Law: Desegregation of the Nation's Public Schools*. Richard Andrews quoted from the case studies of twenty-nine school districts included in the report when he frequently mentioned that most of the best desegregation plans in use in the United States were not equitable. That is, they did not place the burden for student transfers and other inconveniences associated with desegregation equally on the majority and the minority communities. At the first meeting of the No-Name Committee, Shan Mullin referred to the findings of the report concerning the important role civic, business, political and religious leaders play in accomplishing desegregation peacefully. The Church Council often quoted the report to religious leaders to encourage their visible and active support of desegregation efforts. The council also distributed the book widely at workshops (to which leaders in other community organizations were invited, as well as educational leaders in local churches). The council gathered all available copies from the shelves of the local Office of Civil Rights and requested additional copies. Most of the leaders in community organizations involved in efforts to end segregation in Seattle were familiar with this study.

Because Seattle was deeply committed to peaceful desegregation and interested in doing everything possible to accomplish that goal, most of the suggestions in this commission report were followed in Seattle.

Several of the organizations which supported the adoption of the Seattle Plan also provided special services in support of the implementation of the plan.

The Chamber of Commerce, under the leadership of Roy Johnson, made contact with the major radio and TV stations in the area and worked with the school administration to assure that open lines of communication were maintained with the media. A group of community leaders including the superintendent and representatives of the mayor's office, the chamber and the Church Council met with the editorial boards of the television stations to inform television personnel about implementation plans and avenues for obtaining information. Besides the usual information channels available to the press, the superintendent gave his home telephone number to the press and was available to answer questions. The role the media could play in minimizing sensational reporting was discussed along with the important role they could play by disseminating information.

The Church Council, school district and city established a telephone information center and rumor control center in a downtown church. The center was staffed on a 24-hour-a-day basis during the summer and the first few months after the opening of school.

A coalition of community groups under the leadership of Ron Sims coordinated the development of television and radio public service announcements on the subject, "Seattle's Children Are Learning Together," which were aired during the summer before the plan was implemented and during the fall as school was opening. Local businesses contributed to the production costs of the announcements.

Seattle PTSA Council, with the cooperation of the school district, developed a system of bus stop monitors who were stationed at bus stops during the first week of school to assure student safety.

Both the City of Seattle and the school district developed Crisis Intervention and Prevention plans which outlined every conceivable strategy to prevent tension or disruption and an elaborate system of responding to disruption if that should develop. The plan included the assistance of plainclothes police, the Human Rights Department, school conflict-prevention-resolution staff, and security staff. A control center was established in the Municipal Building (City Hall). By 10:00 a.m. on the opening day of school, staff members in the Control Center were bored because they had nothing to do. The elaborate plans were never needed.

The only flaw in the implementation of the Seattle Plan was a teachers' strike which postponed the opening of school two and a half weeks. While this delay produced a considerable amount of frustration for a great many people, it may have been a blessing in disguise because by the time school opened, parents were more eager to have their children back in school than they were worried about the impact of desegregation.

On the opening day of school, Superintendent Moberly flew over the city in a traffic reporting plane and School Board members rode buses, as did the mayor and numerous members of the media. Some buses were late and some children missed buses, but the day was peaceful and carried a note of celebration — "We did it, and did it peacefully!"

The issue of desegregation is not over in Seattle. The constitutionality of State Initiative 350 is still under court review. After the initiative passed, the Seattle, Tacoma and Pasco school districts challenged its constitutionality in federal court. Several community organizations intervened as plaintiffs in the case on the side of the school districts: the ACLU of Washington, the NAACP, the Loren Miller Bar Association (a group of black lawyers), the Seattle Urban League, the Church Council of Greater Seattle, the American Friends Service Committee, and the American Jewish Committee. The Pasco Neighborhood Council also intervened, as did the U.S. Justice Department. Citizens for Voluntary Integration, the drafters of the initiative, intervened in the case on the side of the State of Washington. In the summer of 1979, Judge Donald Voorhees ruled that Initiative 350 was unconstitutional on its face on three grounds. The State of Washington appealed to the Ninth Circuit which affirmed the Voorhees decision by a two-to-one margin in December 1980. Washington State has asked that the entire Ninth Circuit review the case. The court refused to rehear the case. The State of Washington is appealing to the U.S. Supreme Court.

In the meantime, Seattle has completed three years of school under the plan. Student achievement scores as measured by the California Achievement Test have improved (see table 3). Schools are all racially balanced (see table 4, page 184). It will take time to see if the decline in white enrollment in the city, which was taking place before the adoption of the Seattle Plan, will be reversed by the plan.

TABLE 3

Achievement Levels in Seattle Public Schools, 1975 and 1979

Grade Level	CAT 1975	CAT 1979	CAT 1975	CAT 1979	CAT 1975	CAT 1979
	Total Reading		Total Language		Total Math	
1		66		58		65
2	55	57	54	63	58	63
3	59	55	54	54	63	63
4	56	61	51	59	54	63
5	62	65	57	66	62	65
6	62	65	61	64	63	70
7	63	66	57	59	62	67
8	62	64	56	55	64	65

NOTE: In 1975 the tests were administered in the fall; in 1979 they were administered in the spring.

TABLE 4

CHANGES IN RACIAL COMPOSITION OF SCHOOLS, 1976-1980

SCHOOL NAME	MINORITY % 1976-77	MINORITY % 1977-78 (Ex Spec Ed)	MINORITY % Oct., 1980 (62.5 = segregation)		
				WK°	WOK°
Cleveland*	72.8	72.82	63.2		
Franklin*	78.3	76.61	60.5		
Garfield*	72.5	78.42	55.7		
Rainier Beach*	63.8	58.9	54.5		
Mercer*	79.1	80.14	52.1		
Sharples*	75.3	74.89	51.9		
South Shore*	59.4	69.15	51.4		
Beacon Hill*	87.0	85.71		54.5	52.5
Brighton*	87.4	86.93		64.3	60.4
Colman*	94.7	96.03		closed	
Columbia*	74.3	78.22		64.8	61.9
Dearborn Park*	82.5	77.41		56.4	51.5
Dunlap*	77.0	80.60		62.6	61.0
Emerson	46.4	49.00		61.1	62.3
Gatzert*	89.2	91.55		69.1	62.2
Graham Hill*	65.6	63.74		60.5	54.4
Hawthorne*	72.3	72.53		closed	
High Point*	70.0	70.85		62.3	55.3
Kimball*	78.3	87.86 vol.		45.7	46.6
King*	64.4	66.04		49.5	51.4
Leschi*	96.0	90.13		56.3	51.4
Madrona	N.A.	N.A.		58.3	56.0
Maple*	50.7	55.38		57.7	56.6
Minor*	90.8	85.39		54.5	50.6
Muir*	72.9	76.67		57.3	53.6
Rainier View	49.0	49.77		58.5	61.7
Van Asselt*	84.0	84.02		54.5	53.4
Whitworth*	68.4	68.52 vol.		55.2	54.2
Wing Lake*	84.1	86.25		57.1	54.9
Washington	N.A.	N.A.		50.0	50.0

°WK / with kindergarten; WOK / without kindergarten
*Segregated by Board definition, June 1977.

CHAPTER 15

CONCLUSION

How and why Seattle was able to desegregate has been given some thought by many individuals who were involved in the process of developing the Seattle Plan. The question is sometimes expressed as, "What makes Seattle different?" and sometimes as, "What are the five or ten essential factors without which there would be no Seattle Plan?" The questions are not just rhetorical. Seattle did do something which was unique in the more than 25-year history of public school desegregation in the United States. The school district desegregated all of its racially imbalanced schools in three years[1] without one incident of violence, without being ordered to desegregate by a court, and with the support of virtually every organized entity in the city that had any connection with the public schools. Years after the adoption of the plan, numerous individuals were enthusiastic about taking credit for their part in bringing it about.

No discussion of the Seattle Plan would be complete without an attempt to analyze the factors that made Seattle different. The following is one attempt:

1. The threat of a lawsuit was critical.

2. Seattle learned from the past (past mistakes included).

3. Seattle's leaders believed that the city was a good place to live and wanted to keep it that way.

4. Seattle is relatively young and flexible, and its social structure is not set in concrete.

5. Sometimes Seattle is blessed with having the right people available at the right time and place.

6. It helped to talk about it; communication avenues were essential.

7. Maybe we are on the road to "freedom and justice for all" when we do it together.

There would probably not have been a Seattle Plan without the threat of a lawsuit. The legal requirement to desegregate, and the fear of what a court order might do to Seattle, motivated numerous people and groups to support the School Board in its effort to desegregate by its own action. Without the constitutional requirement to remedy public school segregation, there would be no Seattle Plan. The NAACP and the ACLU were primarily responsible for making this fact clear.

Seattle schools were desegregated at a time when there was significant history of desegregation efforts both nationwide and in the city. It was possible to look at past mistakes and attempt to avoid them. Most desegregation efforts throughout the country have not been equitable. Seattle wanted a plan that placed the burden of desegregation equally on the white and racial minority communities. Seattle had experimented with voluntary desegregation, with closing racial minority schools and reassigning those students to predominately white schools (one-way desegregation), and with a voluntary plan with a mandatory backup. All of these plans had their problems. The random assignment notice for the mandatory middle school backup, which parents received by registered mail, evoked an intensely negative emotional response. None of the past desegregation programs in Seattle had kept neighborhood groups of students together, and none had provided parents and students with the security of knowing where students would be attending school each year from kindergarten through grade twelve. In analyses of various approaches to desegregation, these proved to be factors desired by many people. The Seattle Plan meets these two requirements. Though students and their parents still have some choices about schools and programs, those choices are not tied directly to desegregation, but can be made on the basis of the kind of program which best meets the educational needs of students.

Seattleites have always been proud of their city, which is often described as one of the most livable in the country. Community pride and the belief that Seattle could solve local problems probably infected everyone involved in the process of developing the Seattle Plan. Seattle is not affected by the kind of despair or sense of hopelessness that permeates some urban areas. The city is beautiful and is surrounded by some of the most spectacular natural beauty found in the country — towering mountains, clean waterways and luxuriant forests. Seattleites want to keep it that way. Though the city has the potential for succumbing to all of the problems experienced by any urban center, it has usually not failed to address problems before they got out of hand.

There is still a sense in which Seattle is a frontier. There is not a rigid social or political structure which "runs" the city, and while manifestations of racial prejudice are evident, the city considers itself to be relatively tolerant of racial diversity when compared to other areas of the country.

Without attempting to answer the unanswerable question of whether people make history or history makes people, I wish to point out that there were some key individuals involved in the development of the Seattle Plan without whom things might have been quite different. Naming names is difficult, because there were a great many individuals who worked untold hours to bring about the Seattle Plan. Most of their names are included in this book at one place or another. There were a few, however, who were in positions of leadership and were able to use their position in such a way as to help immensely in developing the Seattle Plan. These I shall mention here, without attempting to list them in order of importance. Mayors Wes Uhman and Charles Royer placed the influence of city government squarely behind the School Board and supported desegregation efforts with the resources of the city throughout the implementation of the plan. City government played the most positive role it could have played in the process. The city's desegregation policy was set by Mayor Wes Uhlman for decades to come.

The good political sense and dedicated hard work which Richard Andrews put into his job as chair of the District-Wide Advisory Committee on Desegregation cannot be overstated. Through Andrews's efforts, DWAC became the effective instrument for community involvement in the decision to adopt the Seattle Plan. DWAC was everything a community advisory committee ought to be, and a lot more. The group provided communication links to almost all community organizations that discussed desegregation and to almost all geographic areas of the city. DWAC determined what the nature of the Seattle Plan would be.

Shan Mullin, as president of the Municipal League, spent countless hours keeping the civic and business leadership in Seattle informed on what was happening, and arranged a process for keeping potential adversaries talking to one another in order to prevent open conflict and misunderstanding. Though Mullin would have liked to see a somewhat different desegregation plan for Seattle, his efforts successfully helped keep Seattle "cool."

It might be said that the Urban League planned ahead, and that it's a good idea for someone to have a desegregation plan on the shelf, even if that plan is not used for years. Seattle needed a locally developed desegregation plan which had the blessing of the black and racial minority communities. The Urban League had written one in 1964, and the ability of the Urban League's executive director, Jerome Page, to work effectively with almost all segments of the community helped ensure that the Urban League's plan would become the Seattle Plan. Page served on the board of the Municipal League; the board of the Urban League was chaired by an active member of the Chamber of Commerce. At the same time, the Urban League was clearly tied to the black community. The Urban League could indicate that it would be a plaintiff if there were a suit filed against the school district and simultaneously sign a joint letter from the mayor, the Chamber of Commerce and the Municipal League urging the School Board to take desegregation into its own hands and thereby avoid a court order. The role the Urban League was able to play was to a great extent the result of Jerome Page's personal ability and open style, and the league's hard work.

The most active, indefatigable and hard-working member of the Asian community during the process of developing the Seattle Plan was Arlene Oki. Oki participated in so many community groups that it almost seemed as if she had the ability to be in more than one place at a time. She never let anyone forget that Seattle was desegregating not only its black and white populations, but also its Asian population. Her influence was great.

Clearly there would have been no Seattle Plan if there hadn't been a School Board and superintendent willing to do the job. Of the seven members of the Board, Suzanne Hittman, Dorothy Hollingsworth and Cheryl Bleakney probably took the leadership in desegregation. Suzanne Hittman had been the most clear and open supporter of desegregation and laid much of the groundwork on the Board for the plan. Bleakney took the visible leadership role during the time the plan was being developed. She was effective in this role because she was not as clearly identified a proponent for mandatory desegregation as Hittman was. While Dorothy Hollingsworth, who is black, consciously chose not to take the lead on the Board on desegregation — feeling that segregation was a "white" problem, because it had been caused by whites — her position was always well known and could be counted on. Don Olson's ties to civic and business leaders were essential in order for this segment of the community to feel adequately represented in the process. However, if it had not been for the open and consistent support for mandatory desegregation on Suzanne Hittman's part, it is unlikely that the rest of the School Board would have taken the action it did. Hittman was the cornerstone of the Board's support for desegregation.

And the superintendent was a pragmatist, doing what he was hired to do, desegregating schools the way the School Board and community leaders wanted him to, making his decision on the final plan for Seattle on both political and practical grounds. A "fixed-assignment" plan would get the job of desegregation over and give the district the time to address other issues. Also that was the kind of plan at least three members of the School Board insisted on.

Dick Dyksterhuis was essential to the existence of the Seattle Plan. He wrote it, inspired by a keen sense of the moral need to desegregate, and the need to do it in a just, right and equitable manner. Moberly would describe Dyksterhuis as a "bleeding-heart liberal." It took one to have the courage, imagination and sensitivity to write the Seattle Plan. Dyksterhuis also had the planning skills to do the job. Without him there might have been no plan for the School Board to adopt on December 14, 1977.

And the Church Council of Greater Seattle played a significant role in several ways, initially by defining the philosophical structure around which a plan for Seattle would be developed, by escalating the threat of a lawsuit at the right time to bring the School Board, city government, and the civic and business leadership to the point of facing the decision of how Seattle Public Schools were to be desegregated — through court order or by local action. Finally, it was the council's representative, Ann Siqueland, who made the key motion on the Seattle Plan at DWAC. The Church Council regarded desegregation as a moral issue, and without the council, Seattle's desegregation history would have been different.

Seattle spent considerable time discussing desegregation. This happened in some specific forums, such as the No-Name Committee and DWAC. The discussions were assisted by the newspapers, radio and TV, which provided generally fair and thorough coverage of what was happening. Desegregation was discussed in education committees of numerous organizations, and by the whole community at over thirty informational meetings. It was discussed in over a hundred churches through a Church Council effort, and at several public forums organized by People Power.

When the Declaration of Independence was written, stating that, "All men are created equal and endowed by their creator with certain unalienable rights, and that among these are life, liberty and the pursuit of happiness," that document was referring to white males. Like its English ancestor, the Magna Carta, which initially addressed only the rights of the nobility but later was redefined to address the rights of all English subjects, the U.S. Constitution has been reinterpreted over the years to include the guarantees of equality and justice to individuals who are neither white nor male, and this reinterpretation is a continuing process. The adoption of the Seattle Plan was one manifestation of the change that is taking place in the United States.

Although amendments to prohibit "mandatory busing" of students for desegregation purposes (the only known way of desegregating public schools) are debated in Congress — and although it is possible that the composition of the U.S. Supreme Court could be altered in such a manner that this "court of last resort" might for a time reverse its relatively consistent position, first stated in the 1954 *Brown* decision, of requiring desegregation — it is probably just as unlikely that non-white males will ever again be excluded from constitutional protection as it is that English civil rights will ever revert to being guaranteed only to the nobility. The road only leads in one direction, though the walk is long and painful.

On June 8, 1977, Seattle made a decision to stop discussing whether or not it would desegregate its public schools, and begin discussing *how* it was going to desegregate them. Actually, the scope of that question had changed in the United States in 1954 with the *Brown* v. *Board of Education, Topeka, Kansas*, Supreme Court decision. Seattle took a while to get the message. But it ultimately did get the message that we must recognize our mutual vested interest in working together to guarantee equal rights to everyone. Change is much less painful when we are all working together. And that is the message Seattle is sending back after hearing the message of *Brown*. We did it together.

In various ways all of the individuals and organizations which supported the effort to end segregation in Seattle saw that they had a vested interest in desegregation, whether that interest stemmed from a lifetime of being black or Asian and experiencing firsthand the effects of discrimination, or the concern of a mayor who did not want to invest large amounts of money in police overtime, or the interests of civic leaders in maintaining the ability to make local decisions locally, or the interests of the business community in keeping Seattle economically viable, or the convictions of parents in teaching their children that all people are important, or the knowledge of a superintendent that he must do what four members of a seven-member School Board told him to do, or the wish of those Board members to make their own decisions instead of having someone else tell them what to do. All these decided that it was time to desegregate Seattle Public Schools, rather than fight over the issue of desegregation.

And the process of developing the Seattle Plan was as pure a non-lose decision-making process as the author has ever observed. Of the individuals and groups actively involved, almost all basically got what they wanted. The NAACP wanted the public schools desegregated to the maximum extent possible. This was accomplished without the need for the NAACP to fight a court battle. The Seattle Urban League had also long wanted the public schools desegregated, having written a plan to accomplish the job. The Seattle Plan is basically the Urban League's desegregation plan. The Church Council of Greater Seattle wanted a mandatory desegregation plan that guaranteed equal student transfers and the preservation of ethnic identity. The plan was mandatory and built on the basic principles outlined by the Church Council. Mayor Wes Uhlman, and later Mayor Charles Royer, wanted a desegregation plan that was locally developed, in order to keep the city peaceful and keep local control of the district. The Seattle Plan fulfilled these requirements. The Chamber of Commerce wanted to avoid confrontations over desegregation in order that Seattle would not lose its image as a desirable place to live and work. Desegregation in Seattle produced no identifiable negative impact on the capability of Seattle to maintain a strong economy. The Municipal League of Seattle and King County developed a process for ensuring that as many points of view as possible were represented in the decision-making process, and divisive conflict was avoided. To a very large extent this goal was accomplished.

The Asian community, through its representatives, wanted the multiethnic nature of the city reflected in the plan and wanted minority students represented in schools in sufficient numbers to retain ethnic identity. The dual definition of racial imbalance and the character of the Seattle Plan addresses those concerns. The ACLU wanted significant movement along the road to desegregation. The Seattle Plan was certainly "significant movement." Most community people and parents wanted neighborhood groups of children kept together in school. The plan does that. The superintendent wanted to survive politically in the hostile climate which accompanies desegregation efforts, and not be identified as a "bleeding-heart liberal." Though Superintendent Moberly will always be identified with the Seattle Plan, he did survive the process unscathed, and by those who know him at all well, he will never be viewed as a "bleeding-heart liberal." Though Moberly resigned his position effective summer 1981, he will remain in Seattle as the director of a local foundation. The superintendent found a new home in Seattle.

The Seattle School Board wanted to desegregate, but to avoid the personal trauma past Board members had experienced over desegregation. They got what they wanted. Their action to end segregation in Seattle was accomplished with the largest amount of support from the community which the Board has ever before or since had. They were also able to maintain control of the district and tailor the Seattle Plan to meet the unique characteristics of the city and the school district.

This does not mean that all groups felt they had won or were pleased with the Seattle Plan. The statewide initiative Citizens for Voluntary Integration (CiVIC) sponsored and passed, prohibiting the busing of children beyond their next nearest school for the purpose of desegregation, is evidence of that. In addition, during the month of December 1977, after the Seattle Plan had been released, the school district received numerous letters from the community on the plan. A survey of the school district files revealed that the district received 190 letters opposing the plan and thirty favoring it during this time. Most opponents of the plan disapproved of mandatory busing, wanted neighborhood schools maintained, and feared the loss of the white and middle-class populations. A large percentage of the letters came from the West Seattle and Magnolia Bluff areas of the city, which previous desegregation efforts had not included. One of the letters from West Seattle was a petition with over 100 signatures.

In the summer of 1980, the goal of equal student transfers in the Seattle Plan appeared not to have been reached, as residents of the southeast area of the city complained vehemently to the School Board that their schools were underenrolled because more students had transferred out than were transferring in. The School Board promised to rectify the situation through the new Facilities Plan, adopted in February 1981. The lack of students in southeast area schools is probably the result of the relatively liberal student transfer policies, adopted with the Seattle Plan, which allow students to choose schools other than their assigned ones. This has allowed students to avoid coming into southeast area schools and provided the opportunity for resident southeast area students to transfer to other schools. The complaint from southeast Seattle demonstrates one of the problems with a mandatory desegregation plan with a voluntary backup. It is difficult to administer.

The opportunities for students to transfer from one school to another in Seattle in order to participate in particular programs has provided both the "safety pressure valve" for the otherwise strictly mandatory plan, and some of its biggest administrative headaches. Seattle's white enrollment had been declining for fifteen years prior to the adoption of the Seattle Plan, due to a large extent to declining birth rates and the general aging of the city's population. The Seattle Plan did accelerate middle-class migration for a year or so, but the school population can be expected to stabilize. One reason for this stability is the opportunities for students to choose the schools they will attend if their mandatory assignment doesn't prove satisfactory. Clearly these transfers have to be governed by extensive "student-transfer policies," which have been tightened each year since the adoption of the plan.

There is still much to do in public education in Seattle, and there always will be, but for a while there was time to bask in the knowledge that the job of desegregation had been well done.

Perhaps, by working together, Seattle tasted "freedom and justice for all." In any case, there was something special about the experience of developing the Seattle Plan.

NOTES

INTRODUCTION

1. Elementary buildings which had previously housed kindergarten through grade six would house either kindergarten through grade three or kindergarten and grades four, five and six.
2. Actually the phase-in of the secondary schools required three years to bring all grade levels into compliance.
3. A statewide initiative (Initiative 350) banning the assignment of students beyond their next-nearest school, except for purposes other than desegregation, was passed in 1978. The constitutionality of that initiative is under federal court review.
4. A canal which permits boat traffic to navigate between Lake Washington and Puget Sound.
5. Ordinance 104839, passed by the City Council August 15, 1975.
6. Carol S. Baron, *1977-78 Racial Distribution of Students and Staff*, Seattle Public Schools Report No. 77-27, vol. 1, December 10, 1977. For a comparison of the white to minority percentages of school enrollment in Seattle from 1967 to October 1980, see table 1.

CHAPTER 1

1. *Brown v. Board of Education*, 349 U.S. 294 at 300 (1955).
2. Phillip Burton, interview with author, May 7, May 12, 1980.
3. Bothell is an incorporated city north of Seattle.
4. Burton interview.
5. Burton interview.
6. Burton interview.
7. Burton interview.
8. Central area schools continued to enroll white students up to the time the Seattle Plan was adopted.
9. Burton interview.
10. Patterson became the superintendent of the Baltimore schools after leaving Seattle — the first black superintendent of a major school district.
11. When the Middle School Plan was adopted by the School Board in 1970, it was strictly

196   Notes

        mandatory; later a voluntary recruitment phase was added before mandatory assignments were made.
12. *Seattle Times,* March 22, 1972.
13. Eugene Peterson, "Overview of Seattle's Desegregation History," in *Desegregation: What's Best for All of Our Children,* ed. Ann Siqueland, resource guide and curriculum manual for the Church Council of Greater Seattle, 1977, Session One, pp. 7-9.
14. Most students who transferred for desegregation purposes were black. Many blacks felt the inconveniences of desegregation should be shared by whites. (See table 2, p. 21.)
15. Peterson, "Overview of Seattle's Desegregation History."
16. Pratt lived in the Lake City area of north Seattle. He was shot the evening of January 29, 1969, after answering a knock at the door. His assassin was never found.
17. The original Triad Plan included the socioeconomic integration of the white community as well as the socioeconomic integration of minority and majority communities, because of the belief that socioeconomic factors, rather than racial factors, determine the disadvantaged status of isolated students. There is no necessary advantage to black children who sit in class next to white students. The Seattle Plan is not concerned with socioeconomic integration per se, however.
18. Jerome Page, interview with author, April 25, 1979.
19. Seeking through desegregation to eliminate the isolation of children from low-income homes rather than attempting to have black and white students sit next to one another in a classroom.
20. An agreement between the School Board and the Central Area School Council, giving the latter official advisory power over central area schools.
21. Distar is a particular approach to teaching math and reading.
22. U.S. Department of Health, Education and Welfare.
23. Seattle Public Schools were found to be out of compliance with civil rights assurances school officials had signed to receive funds under Title VII of the Emergency School Aid Act (desegregation funds).
24. Annie Jones, interview with author, October 24, 1980.
25. Jones interview.
26. A nonprofit corporation funded to provide community support for desegregation efforts in Seattle.
27. Jones interview.
28. The Reverend O.J. Moore, interview with author, April 23, 1980.
29. "Official Statement of the Seattle Chapter NAACP on Seattle School Desegregation," quoted in Siqueland, ed., *Desegregation: What's Best for All Our Children?,* 1st ed., Session Five.
30. Lacy Steele, interview with author, June 18, 1980.
31. In 1976 the Office of Civil Rights had ruled that the Seattle Public Schools engaged in this practice. In essence, the truth of this charge had already been proven.
32. "Seattle Branch NAACP vs. Seattle School District No. 1," administrative complaint registered with the U.S. Department of Health, Education and Welfare, Office of Civil Rights, April 20, 1977.

CHAPTER 2

1. Richard Alexander, interview with author, May 7, 1980.
2. Alexander interview.
3. A limit was set on the number and percentage of students of each race who could attend a school.
4. Patt Sutton, interview with author, May 15, 1980.
5. Sutton interview.
6. Citizens for Voluntary Integration, organized just prior to the adoption of the Seattle Plan to oppose mandatory student assignment.
7. Suzanne Hittman, interview with author, July 9, 1979.
8. Ellen Roe, interview with author, July 18, 1979.
9. Roe interview.
10. Dorothy Hollingsworth, interview with author, May 5, 1980.
11. There are two basic approaches to educating a heterogeneous group of students. One is to divide students into achievement level groups and teach each group as a unit. The other approach is to group students intentionally to include diverse achievement levels and then individualize instruction. Because achievement and socioeconomic levels can be correlated, and because race and socioeconomic levels can also be correlated, achievement level grouping can result in segregated grouping. This problem is further complicated by the fact that tests (which determine achievement level) are generally culturally and racially biased. The Middle School Plan attempted to minimize socioeconomic differences between students and racial bias associated with achievement grouping by educating students in intentionally heterogeneous classes.
12. Cheryl Bleakney, interview with author, July 3, 1979.
13. Hittman interview.
14. Sutton interview.
15. The only other levy failure took place in 1959. Levies are submitted twice to the voters (if necessary) and were defeated both times in 1959 and in 1975.
16. The warning predated by a year the filing by the NAACP of a complaint of civil rights violation.
17. *Seattle Times*, May 6, 1976.
18. Dr. David Moberly, interview with author, May 24, July 5, 1979.
19. C. Mike Berry is the president of Seattle First National Bank, the largest bank in the state of Washington.
20. Moberly interview.
21. Seattle School Board Desegregation Committee, "School Board Desegregation Goals, Goal 3: Strategies for Desegregation/Integration," adopted by the School Board May 19, 1976.
22. Hittman interview.
23. Sutton interview.
24. Maynard, who is white, had extensive work experience in multiethnic communities, including Cleveland High School. He had gained the trust of black and Asian community members.
25. The Office of Civil Rights' intended investigation of student-assignment policies, which the district had been notified of in May 1976.
26. Dr. William Maynard, interview with author, April 16, 1979.
27. Maynard interview.
28. Maynard interview.

29. Maynard interview.
30. Maynard interview.
31. Donald Olson, "The Seattle Plan: Pregnancy and Birth," unpublished paper, March 1978, p. 3.
32. Leschi Elementary School went from 96 percent minority in 1976–77 to 87.3 percent minority in 1977–78; Coleman Elementary School was 94.7 percent minority in 1976–77 and 92.3 percent minority in 1977–78; Minor Elementary School went from 90.8 percent minority in 1976–77 to 81.6 percent minority in 1977–78. (Carol S.Baron, N. Allan Boni and Larry Collister, *1976-77 Racial Distribution of Students and Staff*, Seattle Public Schools Report No. 76–25, vol. 1, January 15, 1977.)
33. Five groups of individuals (with some overlap of membership) were involved in various phases of desegregation planning: (1) a "contingency planning team" was organized in March 1977 and included some representatives from DWAC (Patte Poc, Arlene Oki and Barbara Beuschlein); (2) the "technical team" was established in May consisting of Bill Maynard, Art Kono, Dick Dyksterhuis, Jim Page, Bob Hamilton and DWAC's representative Patte Poc. Ricky Malone joined the group in mid-June; (3) the "contingency team" consisted of Bill Maynard, Dan Riley, Dick Dyksterhuis, Bob Hamilton, Mako Nakagawa, Tony Orange from the administration and Cheryl Crawford, Barbara Beuschlein, Arlene Oki and Patte Poc from DWAC; (4) a "steering team" met weekly with the technical team and included Dave Colwell, Jr., the regional administrators and two building principals; (5) the "writing group" which wrote the desegregation plan included Ricky Malone, Patte Poc, Dick Dyksterhuis, Bob Hamilton and Jim Page. Hamilton and Page did not participate in the writing of the final Seattle Plan.
34. Moberly described himself this way when he arrived in Seattle.
35. Patte Poc, interview with author, July 10, 1979.

CHAPTER 3

1. Levant, who is white, originally represented the Central Area School Council on DWAC. CASC has never been an exclusively black group.
2. Dan Levant, interview with author, February 17, 1979.
3. Levant interview.
4. Levant interview.
5. Levant interview.
6. Levant interview.
7. Levant interview.
8. Dan Levant is not black.
9. Dr. Richard Andrews, interview with author, March 28, 1979.
10. Andrews interview.
11. The school district had surveyed parents to decide what kind of programs to include in the Magnet Plan.
12. Andrews interview.
13. Andrews interview.

CHAPTER 4

1. Lau v. Nichol, 414 U.S. 563 (1974).
2. Don Kazama, interview with author, January 17, 1979.
3. Arlene Oki, interview with author, June 19, 1979.
4. Contained in Title VII Emergency School Aid Act guidelines.
5. The Voluntary Racial Transfer Steering Committee, a subcommittee of DWAC, disbanded in early 1977 when its chair, Bea Schott, resigned, totally frustrated with the lack of support for voluntary recruitment in the district.
6. Royer was then working for KING-TV and was PTSA president at Eckstein Middle School; currently he is mayor of Seattle.
7. Oki interview.
8. High school area advisory committees were formed in all areas of the city following the formation of the Central Area School Council. All have disbanded except for CASC.
9. Sam Shoji, interview with author, July 2, 1979.
10. Shoji interview.
11. Arthur Miller was flown in to teach creative writing.
12. Shoji interview.
13. Gary Higashi, interview with author, June 14, 1979.
14. Higashi interview.

CHAPTER 5

1. The Reverend Donald S. Daughtry, "A New Vision of Racial Justice in Education," sermon delivered at the Beacon Avenue United Church of Christ, Seattle, summer 1976.
2. The threat of a full-scale civil rights investigation by the Office of Civil Rights, which the district had received in May 1976.
3. "Statement on the Desegregation of Seattle Schools," adopted by the Church Council of Greater Seattle December 14, 1976.
4. Ibid.
5. Ibid.
6. Ibid.
7. The Reverend Dr. William Cate, interview with author, July 11, 1979.
8. The Reverend Don Daughtry, interview taped by Roger Hagen and Associates in Hawaii, May 2, 1979.
9. Cate interview.
10. Oki interview.
11. The two School Board threshold criteria were equalization of student transfers and maintaining ethnic identity.
12. The Reverend Dr. David Colwell, Sr., interview with author, May 5, 1980.

CHAPTER 6

1. Each high school had an advisory committee for a time during the early 1970s. These committees developed in response to the Central Area School Council.
2. Beuschlein preceded Groves as council president; she was elected to the Seattle School Board in 1979.
3. Kay Groves, interview with author, June 18, 1979.
4. Chair of the Church Council's Task Force on Racial Justice in Education, which developed the Church Council's desegregation position.
5. Groves interview.
6. Barbara Beuschlein resides in the Ravenna Elementary School area; Kay Groves in the Broadview Elementary area.
7. Letter to Ann Siqueland from Austrid Hedman, president, Seattle League of Women Voters, July 29, 1977, p. 1.
8. School district administrators charged with desegregation planning.
9. Letter to the Seattle School Board from the League of Women Voters, December 8, 1976.
10. The Rowntree Money was a bequest to the League of Women Voters of Seattle from Jennie Rowntree.
11. Austrid Hedman, interview with author, June 15, 1979.
12. Letter to the Seattle School Board from the League of Women Voters, May 25, 1977.
13. Jonis Davis, interview with author, June 29, 1979.
14. Davis interview.
15. Davis interview.
16. Davis interview.
17. Arlis Stewart, interview with author, June 18, 20, 1979.
18. Stewart interview.
19. Stewart interview.
20. From the Center for National Policy Review, Washington, D.C.
21. Stewart interview.
22. Stewart interview.

CHAPTER 7

1. Dan Levant, interview with author, February 17, 1979.
2. Fred Noland, interview with author, August 12, 1980.
3. Seattle School Board Desegregation Committee, "School Board Desegregation Goals, Goal 3: Strategies for Desegregation/Integration," adopted by the School Board May 19, 1976.
4. Memo to ACLU Board of Directors from ACLU School Desegregation Committee, re: Recommendations for Implementation of ACLU Position (no date; after July 1976), p. 1.
5. Noland interview.
6. Noland interview.
7. Noland interview.
8. David Harrison, taped recollections, July 1980.
9. Noland interview.

10. Noland interview.
11. Angelos is the *Seattle Times* editor; Nalder covered school issues for the *Seattle Post-Intelligencer* at the time. The *Times* and the *P.-I.* are Seattle's only large daily newspapers.
12. Harrison tape.
13. Memo to David Harrison, Fred Noland, Dan Levant and Ann Siqueland from Annette Klapstein, re: 8/21/77 Meeting — "Where Are We, and Where Do We Go From Here?" (no date), p. 1.

CHAPTER 8

1. Mayor Wesley Uhlman, interview with author, September 4, 1980.
2. Uhlman interview.
3. Uhlman interview.
4. Uhlman interview.
5. Uhlman interview.
6. Memo to Wes Uhlman, mayor, from R.W. Wilkinson, director, Office of Policy Planning, re: School Desegregation Impacts for Seattle, February 8, 1977.
7. Ibid.
8. Dr. David Moberly, interview with author, May 24, July 5, 1979.
9. Uhlman interview.
10. Uhlman interview.
11. The nine members of the Seattle City Council are elected on a nonpartisan basis (as is the mayor) for at-large positions.
12. Shelly Yapp, interview with author, May 2, 1980.
13. Uhlman interview.
14. Yapp interview.
15. Uhlman interview.
16. Letter to Don Olson, president, Seattle School Board, from the Municipal League, the Chamber of Commerce, the city of Seattle and the Urban League, May 20, 1977.
17. Uhlman interview.
18. Yapp interview.

CHAPTER 9

1. Patt Sutton, interview with author, May 15, 1980.
2. *Fulfilling the Letter and Spirit of the Law: Desegregation of the Nation's Public Schools*, report of the U.S. Commission on Civil Rights, August 1976.
3. The chair of the chamber's Education Committee preferred not to discuss desegregation.
4. Shan Mullin, interview with author, July 26, 1979.
5. Draft of Municipal League resolution, January 21, 1976.
6. Letter from C. Mike Berry to Don Olson, July 18, 1977.

Notes

7. Russ Amick, interview with author, June 7, 1979.
8. Amick interview.
9. Amick interview.
10. Amick interview.
11. Shelly Yapp, interview with author, May 2, 1980.
12. Amick interview.
13. Yapp interview.
14. Jerry Skutt, interview with author, August 9, 1979.
15. Two other members of the Municipal League's Education Committee, Carol Richman and Arlis Stewart, also served on DWAC.
16. With the exception of Skutt, all of these individuals are members of the board of the Chamber of Commerce.
17. Rob Makin recalls being at the meeting. Skutt recalls that Fred Evans was present instead of Makin.
18. Skutt interview.
19. Rob Makin, interview with author, July 6, 1979.
20. Letter to Don Olson, president, Seattle School Board, from the Municipal League, the Chamber of Commerce, the city of Seattle and the Urban League, May 20, 1977.
21. Ibid.
22. Mayor Uhlman expected a mandatory component would be included in a desegregation plan; however, at that point Amick believed Uhlman did not expect that outcome.
23. Amick interview.
24. Amick interview.
25. Skutt interview.
26. Makin interview.
27. Mullin interview.
28. Eben Carlson, interview with author, July 2, 1979.
29. Suzanne Hittman, interview with author, July 9, 1979.
30. Cheryl Bleakney, interview with author, July 3, 1979.
31. Bleakney interview.
32. Bleakney interview.
33. Don Olson, interview with author, July 24, 1979.
34. Dr. David Moberly, interview with author, May 24, July 5, 1979.
35. Black, Asian American, Hispanic, Native American.
36. Seattle School Board Resolution 1977-8, adopted June 8, 1977.
37. Dorothy Hollingsworth, interview with author, May 6, 1980. Hollingsworth's insistence that racial imbalance be *eliminated* continued. Largely because of her insistence, the Board took action in January of 1978 to intervene in schools which were not racially balanced in the first year of the plan. Her concern may have been even more of a deciding factor in 1978 than in 1977.
38. Seattle School Board Minutes, June 1, 1977, p. 20.
39. The League of Women Voters suggested forty percent single minority, sixty percent combined minority and fifty percent plus-or-minus ten percent in some specific instances. Statement to members of the Seattle School Board from the League of Women Voters, June 8, 1977.
40. The vote on the definition of racial imbalance at the Board meeting came after a confrontation between Dorothy Hollingsworth and Arlene Oki. This confrontation pointed out the need for better lines of communication between the black and Asian

communities. A series of "black and yellow" meetings was held following the June 8 meeting, to address this need.
41. Bleakney interview.
42. Sutton interview.

CHAPTER 10

1. Seattle Public Schools, *Proposed Alternative Desegregation Plans*, published report, September 1977.
2. The May 11 meeting was the same meeting at which Cheryl Bleakney introduced a resolution committing the Board to define and eliminate racial imbalance.
3. Cheryl Bleakney, interview with author, July 3, 1979.
4. This fact became apparent by reaction to the Seattle Plan in November. A tremendous amount of work was undertaken by DWAC members and the administration to keep the public informed. The media were very cooperative. However, a great many people still appeared to be surprised in November.
5. Not everyone on the School Board or DWAC would agree; however, the Seattle Plan does not include a specific educational philosophy.
6. Dr. David Moberly, interview with author, May 24, July 5, 1979.
7. The assignment patterns of elementary school attendance areas to junior high, middle school and high school.
8. A School Board attempt to close schools in 1974 was postponed by a lawsuit. Several schools were closed in 1981.
9. The School Board has made a commitment to rebuild Hawthorne as soon as funds are available.

CHAPTER 11

1. Resolution of the board of directors of the ACLU of Washington, June 4, 1977.
2. The largest portion of this money came from the United Church of Christ.
3. The Reverend Dr. William Cate, interview with author, July 11, 1979.
4. The Reverend Dr. David Colwell, Sr., interview with author, May 5, 1980.
5. Eben Carlson took over that role in March 1978.
6. Dr. Richard Andrews, interview with author, May 14, 1980.
7. Shan Mullin, interview with author, July 26, 1979.
8. Nand Hart-Nibbring, "Policies of School Desegregation in Seattle," *Washington Public Policy Notes*, ed. Susie Anschell (Institute of Government Research, University of Washington), vol. 7, no. 1 (1979).
9. Gary Higashi, interview with author, June 14, 1979.

CHAPTER 12

1. Dr. William Maynard, interview with author, April 6, 1979.
2. Dr. David Moberly, interview with author, May 24, July 5, 1979.
3. Options were magnet-type educational programs to which students could transfer; the Board had made a three-year commitment to maintain magnet-type programs in the district. It is difficult to figure out how to administer a desegregation plan which mandatorily assigns students and then lets them voluntarily move to magnet options.
4. Cheryl Bleakney, interview with author, July 3, 1979. Moberly had asked the School Board to renew his contract in September. The Board voted four-to-three to do that, with Hollingsworth voting in favor of the renewal.
5. Voluntary plans allowed students to choose a variety of schools to attend, and students in a particular neighborhood would be expected to "scatter" as they had during the past under the voluntary racial transfer plan.
6. The term "fixed-assignment" became a code word for a desegregation plan that was based on the mandatory reassignment of students, such as the Urban League's Triad Plan.
7. Rob Makin, interview with author, July 6, 1979.
8. Movement between buildings would make it more difficult to insure racial balance; exemplary programs should be provided to enhance schools involved in pairs and triads.
9. Hamilton had not attended the meeting called by Moberly; Core Committee members, however, did not know that on November 9.
10. On November 2 the School Board had given Moberly permission to bring only one final plan instead of two.
11. DWAC Minutes, November 7, 1977, p. 2, item IV (a): "DWAC must make some resolution about the final plan on November 9 so that the DPO [District Planning Office] can complete writing by the 17th, turn the plan over to DWAC by the 22nd, and give it to the Board on December 1."
12. Dr. Richard Andrews, interview with author, March 28, 1979.
13. Barbara Beuschlein, interview with author, May 12, 1980.
14. Jerry Skutt, interview with author, January 2, 1981.
15. Skutt interview.
16. Russ Amick, interview with author, June 7, 1979.
17. Andrews interview.
18. Skutt interview.
19. This Board action was taken on November 2. Shan Mullin recalls that the superintendent had previously promised the community that he would deliver two plans to the Board; the change created some dissatisfaction, especially in Mullin and the Municipal League.
20. Bleakney interview.
21. This came after Cheryl Bleakney and Dick Andrews told the superintendent "he had an insurrection" on his hands.
22. Richard Dyksterhuis, interview with author, May 29, 1979.
23. Dyksterhuis interview.
24. Andrews interview.

CHAPTER 13

1. The Seattle Plan does not include kindergarten.
2. Constance Herring, statement to the Seattle School Board, November 16, 1977.
3. CASC, statement to the Seattle School Board, December 7, 1977.
4. Jerome Page, statement to the Seattle School Board, December 5, 1977.
5. Dr. Richard Andrews, interview with author, May 14, 1980.
6. Sidney Freeman, interview with author, January 15, 1979.
7. Freeman interview.
8. Shelly Yapp, interview with author, May 2, 1980.
9. Andrews interview.
10. Mayor Charles Royer, interview with author, September 4, 1980.
11. Royer interview.
12. Joint statement from Mayor Uhlman and Mayor-elect Royer, delivered by Woody Wilkinson to the Seattle School Board, December 5, 1977.
13. Rob Makin, interview with author, July 6, 1979.
14. Makin interview.
15. Makin interview.
16. Makin interview.
17. Russ Amick, interview with author, June 7, 1979.
18. Makin interview.
19. Amick interview.
20. Seattle School Board, "Tasks, Responsibilities and Timeline for Completion of Desegregation Plans," report, October 26, 1977.
21. Memo to David Moberly from William Maynard, November 2, 1977.
22. This kind of open debate never took place publicly at School Board meetings.
23. "Municipal League Position on Desegregation," unpublished paper, November 21, 1977.
24. Andrews interview.
25. Arlis Stewart, interview with author, June 18, 20, 1979.
26. Jonis Davis, interview with author, June 29, 1979.
27. Susan Wallace, interview with author, November 5, 1980.
28. Wallace interview.
29. Students can voluntarily choose to attend "all-school magnets" in schools which are not paired or triaded; Kimball, Laurelhurst and Whitworth are examples.
30. Don Olson, interview with author, July 24, 1979.
31. The narrative does not include the names of schools participating in the plan; instead, it contains the educational, historical and philosophical content of the plan.
32. Andrews interview.
33. *Seattle Times*, December 6, 1977.
34. Suzanne Hittman, interview with author, July 9, 1979.

CHAPTER 14

1. Cheryl Bleakney statement, Seattle School Board Minutes, December 14, 1977.
2. Richard Alexander statement, Seattle School Board Minutes, December 14, 1977.
3. Dorothy Hollingsworth statement, Seattle School Board Minutes, December 14, 1977.
4. Ellen Roe statement, Seattle School Board Minutes, December 14, 1977.
5. Suzanne Hittman statement, Seattle School Board Minutes, December 14, 1977.
6. Patt Sutton statement, Seattle School Board Minutes, December 14, 1977.
7. Don Olson statement, Seattle School Board Minutes, December 14, 1977.
8. Dr. Richard Andrews, interview with author, May 14, 1980.
9. Luther Lund became chair of DWAC in the summer of 1979. Lund became involved in DWAC through activities in the triad his daughter attends (Wedgwood/Decatur/Leschi).
10. Letter to Don Olson from the Municipal League of Seattle and King County, December 14, 1977.
11. Ibid.
12. Shan Mullin, interview with author, July 26, 1979.
13. Agenda for Desegregation Coordination Group, February 23, 1978, meeting.
14. "Joint Statement of Seattle Black Community Leaders" No. C78-753V, Seattle School District No. 1 et al v. The State of Washington et al, U.S. District Court, Western District of Washington, 1979.
15. Dan Levant, interview with author, February 17, 1979.
16. David Harrison, taped recollections, July 1980.
17. Mayor Wesley Uhlman, interview with author, September 4, 1980.
18. Mayor Charles Royer, interview with author, September 4, 1980.

CHAPTER 15

1. In October 1980, Cleveland High School was out of racial balance by two students; all other schools in the district are racially balanced. See table 4.

INDEX

Alexander, Richard, 3, 13, 25-26, 165, 171
American Civil Liberties Union of Washington, 177, 191, and Chapter 7
    in Initiative 350 Suit, 182
    membership in DWAC, 42
    participation in No-Name Committee, 131
    review of School Board resolutions by, 119
    threats of desegregation lawsuit by, 60, 82, 93, 95, 97, 113, 127
American Friends Service Committee, 73, 78-80, 161-162, 182
American Jewish Committee, 182
Amick, Russ, 105-107, 109, 111-112, 130, 132, 157-158
Andrews, Barbara, 48, 141, 150, 179, 180
Andrews, Richard, 160, 179-180, 187
    regarding City of Seattle recommendation, 153
    on December 14, 1977, 173-174
    in development of final DWAC recommendation, 139-146
    regarding DWAC criteria, 120, 48-49
    "just, right and equitable," 133
    regarding the No-Name Committee, 130, 132
    in writing the Seattle Plan, 149-150, 166-168
Apodaca, Alan, 35
Angelos, Constantine (Gus), 91, 166, 168
Asian American Education Association, 56-61, 128, 177

Balderama, Virginia, 69
Berry, C. Mike, 33, 105, 108, 110
Beuschlein, Barbara, 51, 75, 143, 149
Bilingual Advisory Committe, 54
Bilingual education, 31, 53, 54, 169
Black employment in Seattle, 10
Black United Clergy for Action, 20, 21, 64, 73

Bleakney, Cheryl
    background of, 28, 30, 34
    in Board's desegregation criteria, 120-121
    in December 14, 1977 vote, 4, 165, 170-171
    defining racial imbalance, 118
    DWAC meeting, attendance at, 142, 143
    efforts of, to initiate Seattle Plan, 111, 113-114, 188
    in Initiative 350, 179
    in negotiations with HEW, 18
    Seattle Plan, position on, 137-138, 147
Bottomly, Forbes, 13, 14, 29-31, 40
Bowns, Carmella, 34, 114
Boycott of Seattle schools, 12
Brewster, David, 147
Brown v. Board of Education, 9-10, 16, 53, 86, 190
Brown, Linda, 9
Brown, Oliver, 9
Bullitt, Katherine, 130
Burdell, Charles, 11
Bundy, Emory, 80
Bunn, Wallace R., 102, 105, 112, 157, 158
Burton, Phillip, 10-12, 23, 88

Cameron, Peggy, 28, 30
Carlson, Eben, 83, 105, 109, 112, 132, 160
Carlson, Nancy, 70
Cate, William, 64, 66-68, 72, 80, 129
Central Area Civil Rights Committee, 14, 64, 67
Central Area School Council (CASC), 13
    early desegregation efforts of, 15, 17-19, 22
    in January 3, 1977 meeting with School Board, 37
    membership in DWAC, 42
    Seattle Plan, position on, 44, 152
Chamber of Commerce, Seattle, 4, 33, 52, 73, 191, and Chapter 9

208 Index

assistance of, in implementing the plan, 181
joint letter of, 101-102
Seattle Plan, position on, 156-158
Church Council of Greater Seattle, 189, 191, and Chapter 5
assistance of, in implementing the plan, 180-182
BUCFA, working with, 20
education program of, 70-71
litigation by, 60, 71-73, 92, 113, 127-129
membership in DWAC, 42, 44
Seattle Plan, position on, 143, 164
statement on desegregation, 20, 64-70, 117-118
Christian Friends for Racial Equality, 10
Citizens Against Mandatory Busing (CAMB), 13, 14, 28, 75, 124
Citizens' Committee for Quality Education (CCQE), 26
Citizens for Voluntary Integration (CiVIC), 4, 26, 158, 179, 182, 192
Civic Unity Committee, 10
Civil rights complaint, 1977, by the NAACP, 23-24
Cleveland High School, 35, 57
Closure of schools, 126, 164
Coalition for Quality Integrated Education (CQIE), 19, 40, 42, 55, 64
Colwell, David, Sr., 26, 70, 71, 129, 130, 132
Committee for Southeast Seattle Schools, 44, 56, 64
Cooper, Mark, 102, 105, 108-111
Cornelius, John, 21, 66
Cowles, Alfred, 14, 25, 29
Crawford, Cheryl, 17, 51, 134, 135, 139, 149, 167

Daughtry, Don, 62-63, 70, 75
Davis, Jonis, 51, 78-80, 161, 162
Dewitty, Thelma, 10
District-Wide Advisory Committee on Desegregation (DWAC), 173-174, and Chapter 3
as communications network, 133-134
defining racial imbalance, 118
desegregation criteria of, 48-49, 120-121
disbanding of, 51-52
final plan presented to, 166
final recommendation of, 139-143
in January 3, 1977, meeting with School Board, 37-38, 44
Magnet Plan, analysis of, 49-50
membership of, 42-44, 50-51
planning models to, 125-126
Dorse, Robert, 26

Duff, George, 102
Dunphy, Mary Elayne, 113
Dyksterhuis, Richard, 36-37, 113, 136, 141
during writing of the Seattle Plan, 147-150, 164, 189

Elskie, Kathy, 51
Eckstein Middle School, 14, 112
Emergency School Aid Act, Title VII, 40, 53, 67, 117
Executive Order 9066, 58

Fair Employment Practices Act of Washington State, 1949, 10
4-4-4 Plan, 13
Filipino Teachers Association, 56
Fixed-assignment concept, 121, 152, 159, and Chapter 12
Franklin High School, 11
Freeman, Sidney, 51, 110, 114, 153-154
Fulfilling the Spirit and Letter of the Law, 180

Garfield High School, 10, 41
Gayton, Carver, 29
Gillespie, Cynthia, 88, 93
Ginsberg, Phillip, 88, 93
Goe, Mary Ann, 51
Gossett, Larry, 175
Groves, Kay, 44, 51, 74-75, 149, 162

Haley, Don, 93
Hamilton, Bobby, 141
Harrison, David, 72, 89-93, 109, 177
Hasegawa, Hilo, 50, 59
Hay Elementary School, 84
Hayasaka, Phillip, 64
Haynes, Grover, 50
Health, Education and Welfare, Department of, 18, 35, 53, 55-56, 62-63, 87, 97
Hedman, Astrid, 77
Herring, Constance, 15, 44, 50, 93, 109, 139, 151
Higashi, Gary, 59-61, 128, 135, 177
Hittman, Suzanne
background of, 26-27
bilingual programs, attitude toward, 169
and Board desegregation goals, 34
in December 14, 1977 vote, 4, 172
defining voluntary transfer, 32
lawsuit, position on, 91
Seattle Plan, position on, 139, 147, 165
support of desegregation by, 111, 113, 188-189
Hollingsworth, Dorothy
background of, 28-29

Church Council, meeting with, 64
  in December 14, 1977 vote, 4, 171
  defining racial imbalance, 135
  Seattle Plan, position on, 147, 165, 188
  support of desegregation by, 111, 113
Horace Mann Elementary School, 107
Houser, Bertha, 88
Housing integration, 5, 10-11, 16, 27
Houston, John, 54
Hubbard, Walter, 64, 67

Initiative 350, 175, 177, 179, 180, 182
Interlake Elementary School, 107
In Touch, 56
Iwamoto, Edward, 66
Iwamoto, Gary, 128-130

Jamero, Peter, 64
Japanese American Citizens League, 56-59, 73, 177
Johnson, Charles, 67, 93
Johnson, Roy, 181
Joint letter, 101-103, 109-111, and Chapter 9
Jones, Annie, 17-19, 50
Justice Department, U.S., 182

Kazama, Don, 54, 55, 59
King, Ivan, 134
Klapstein, Annette, 92
Kumasaka, Jan, 51, 59
Kvamme, Olaf, 99, 102, 130, 153

Laurelhurst Elementary School, 111-112
Lau v. *Nichol* (U.S. Supreme Court Decision), 53
League of Women Voters, 4, 28, 73
  defining racial imbalance, 118
  desegregation efforts of, 76-78
  DWAC involvement of, 42-44
  in Initiative 350, 179
  Seattle Plan, position on, 138-139, 164
Lemley, Tom, 128
Levant, Dan, 177
  ACLU, work with, 86
  as DWAC chair, 37-38, 43-44, 56-57
  Moberly, meeting with, 44-45
  resignation of, 46-47
Levy, school funding, 8, 26, 31, 104
Lindquist, Reese, 51
Little, Gary, 32, 34, 41, 90, 118
Local control of schools, 4, 179
Loren Miller Bar Association, 182
Lutheran Church in America, 65
Lydle, Dean & Marylyn, 50

Malone, Ricky, 38, 147

Magnet Plan, 22, 35, 77, 107, 112, 121
  problems with, 38-39, 46, 57, 100, 115, 138
Makin, Rob, 51, 110, 112, 156-158
Mathews, Henrietta, 64, 175
Mathews, Meredith, 67
Maynard, William
  appointed desegregation director, 35-37
  in City of Seattle presentation, 101
  regarding continuum, 121-123
  DWAC, working with, 45, 49
  final plan of, 136-137, 141, 167
  memo regarding one plan versus two, 159
McKinney, Samuel, 175
Meany-Madrona Middle School, 13, 112, 117
Media, news, 80-82, 123, 139, 147, 164-166, 168, 181, 189
Middle School Desegregation Plan, 13-15, 27-31, 111-112, 124
Moberly, David
  hiring of, 22, 32, 44-45, 104-105
  initial desegregation efforts of, 32, 115
  middle school plan, attitude toward, 124-125
  during opening day of Seattle Plan, 182
  Seattle Plan, position on, 32-34, 137, 158, 166-168, 189
Moore, O. J., 20-21
Mullin, J. Shan, 187
  attempts of, to avoid a lawsuit, 83, 106, 129
  involvement in joint letter, 108-112
  as No-Name Committee member, 130-132, 175, 180
  in "process" of developing Seattle Plan, 158-161
  Seattle Plan, position on, 165, 168
Municipal League of Seattle and King County, 4, and Chapter 9
  during community review period, 173-175
  desegregation, position on, 160
  membership in DWAC, 50
  Seattle Plan, position on, 157-161, 165, 187, 191
Murray, Cecil, 21, 64, 66, 67, 71, 72

Nalder, Eric, 91, 113, 168
National Association for the Advancement of Colored People (NAACP), 191
  in Initiative 350 Suit, 182
  national efforts of, 9-10
  membership in DWAC, 15, 42, 44
  in OCR complaint, 22-24
  reviewing School Board Resolution, 119
  threatening desegregation lawsuit, 60, 93, 95, 97, 109, 113

210   Index

Noland, Fred, 73, 86, 88-90, 92, 93, 109, 128
No-Name Committee (Desegregation Coordinating Group), 130-133
    as communication link, 91, 123, 124, 180, 189
    in final Seattle Plan, 157, 175

Office of Civil Rights, Region X, 22, 31-32, 69, 71, 181
Office of Policy Planning of City of Seattle, 94, 97-99, 110
Ogilvie, Tony, 64
Oki, Arlene, 188
    as Asian community representative, 55-57, 184
    involvement in Church Council, 63-64, 68
    involvement in DWAC, 43, 44, 50, 139, 149
Olson, Donald, 130, 145, 188
    background of, 28
    as Chamber of Commerce liaison, 102
    in December 14, 1977 vote, 4, 172-173
    in establishment of DWAC, 42
    in final Seattle Plan, 165-166, 168
    hiring Moberly, 32
    in January 3, 1977 meeting, 37-38
    regarding joint letter, 111, 114, 115
Orange, Tony, 18, 64

Page, James, III, 37-38
Page, Jerome, 188
    in black and Asian communications, 135
    and black coalition, 139, 151, 175
    finding chair for DWAC, 47, 48
    in final Seattle Plan, 152
    regarding joint letter, 103, 110
    as No-Name Committee participant, 132
    and Urban League approach to desegregation, 16-17
Palmason, Edward, 25
Parent, Teacher, Student Association, Seattle Council (PTSA), 74-76
    membership in DWAC, 42, 44
    Seattle Plan, position on, 162-164, 181
Patterson, Roland, 13
Patti, Nadine, 51
Payne, Ancil, 109
People Power Coalition, 80-85, 91, 106, 114
    forums of, 123, 189
Plan "A," 147
Poc, Patti, 38, 39, 50, 147, 148, 162
Pratt, Edwin, 12, 15

Racial imbalance, definition of
    by Asian community, 56, 68
    by black community, 15, 20, 67
    by Church Council, 20, 66-70, 117-118
    by DWAC, 118
    by H.E.W., 62-63
    by League of Women Voters, 118
    by NAACP, 118
    in Seattle School Board Resolution, 116-119, 127, 135
    by Urban League, 118
Recall of Seattle School Board attempted, 30, 31
Rockefeller, Phillip, 35
Richman, Carol, 51
Rhone, Jonathan, 64
Reasby, Harold, 36, 87
Roe, Ellen, 34, 165
    background of, 27-28
    in December 14, 1977 vote, 4, 171
    defining voluntary desegregation, 32
    encouraging opponents of mandatory desegregation, 124
    PTSA involvement of, 74-75
Roosevelt High School, 14
Royer, Charles, 57, 154-156, 179, 187, 191

School Board, Seattle, 3-4, 113-119, 188-189, and Chapter 2
    in December 14, 1977 vote, 3-4, 170-173
    desegregation goals of, 87
    desegregation committee of, 34
    desegregation criteria of, 120-121
    Resolution 1974-14 of, 41
    Resolution 1977-8/9 of, 116-119
Scott, Charles, 9
Seattle, City of, 5-8, 52, 110, 119, 181, and Chapter 8
Seattle Plan for the Elimination of Racial Imbalance
    adoption of, 3-4, 170-177
    analysis of, 185-193
    black community attitude toward, 15, 19
    criteria for, 119-121
    enabling resolutions (1977-8/9) for, 116-119
    final draft of, 166-168
    joint letter signers' attitude toward, 111-112
    proposed alternatives to, 125
    public hearings on, 126, 138, 155, 156, 168-169
    reactions to, 164-166
    writing of, 136-150
Seattle Teachers Association, 4, 123, 182
Segregation, illegal, 26, 34-35, 90-92, 107
Shoji, Sam, 50, 56-59, 177
Sims, Ron, 181
Skutt, Jerry, 50, 108-110, 112, 139-146, 167

Siqueland, Ann
   Church Council activities of, 66, 70, 72, 128, 189
   DWAC activities of, 42, 51, 139, 142-144, 167
Smith, Beverly, 25, 30
Smith, Charles Z., 175
Smith, Donald, 93
Steele, Lacy, 22, 23, 72, 109, 175
Stevens, Fred, 175
Stewart, Arlis, 114, 134, 142, 160-161, 168
   DWAC activities of, 51, 149, 167
   People Power activities of, 81-85
Stewart, Joan, 64
Student Action Force on Education, 78-80, 161, 162
Supreme Court, U.S., 9, 53
Supreme Court, Washington State, 7, 14, 30, 190
Sutton, Patt, 119, 130
   background of, 26, 30, 31, 41
   in December 14, 1977 vote, 4, 172
   in final Seattle Plan, 165
   illegal segregation, position on, 34-35
Swain, Phillip, 25

Thompson, Robert, 109
Tidwell, Robert, 25, 28, 30
Title VII Advisory Committee, 42, 55, 64
Triad Plan, 12, 28, 118, 125, 133, 145-147, 156, 158
   effect of, on socio-economic desegregation, 15-17, 134, 135
Troxel, Loren, 31, 40, 43
Tyler, Jim, 88

Uhlman, Wesley
   in joint letter, 108, 110
   relationship of, with Moberly, 33
   and role of city government in desegregation, 94-103, 187, 191
   Seattle Plan, position on, 178
   in transition of mayoralty, 154, 155
Urban League, Seattle
   desegregation approach of, 15-17
   in joint letter, 101, 110
   litigation by, 93, 182
   membership in DWAC, 51
   Seattle Plan, position on, 152, 187-188, 191
   regarding Triad Plan. *See* Triad Plan

Voluntary Racial Transfer Program, 11, 17, 21, 22, 27, 40-41, and Table 2
Voluntary Racial Transfer Steering Committe, 42
Voorhees, Donald, 182

Wagoner, David, 25, 28, 30
Wallace, Susan, 51, 56, 162-164
Washington Association of Churches, 54
White, Kevin, 96
Wilkins, William J., 13
Wilkinson, J. (Woody), 96-100, 152, 154, 155, 156
Williams, Peg, 76
Williams, Walt, 130
Woods, Fabiola, 51

Yapp, Shelly, 90, 100, 102, 114, 132, 152-154
Youngman, Judith, 50, 56

Zarter, Ellen, 51
Zoning, 125, 157